# CAMPUS PLACEMENT GUIDE FOR MANAGEMENT TRAINEE IN LEADING HOTELS

DR ANSHUMALI PANDEY

# Contents

# Foreword

*Question:*

*When is the right time to start preparing for the Campus
Placement?*

*Answer:*

*Today.*

# Preface

In my over 26 years of Hospitality Management Experience primarily with the IHMs and Central Government projects, I have observed that the Hotel management students are usually very clear with their objectives and goals. Hence it is seen that they start preparing for the eventual Campus Placements from the first semester itself.

This book shall help those students who are serious about bagging the coveted Management Trainee (MT) batch of leading Hospitality Groups through Campus Placements. It is important to grab the best job in the industry as a good launch pad helps the newcomers to catapult themselves higher ranks in a shorter span.

This book comprises of researched resource materials, tips and skills required by the hospitality students to glide through success in attaining a Management Trainee assignment. This book is divided systematically into the three major subjects required for a MT job, i.e. F&B Service, Front Office and House Keeping. As far as Kitchen Trainees is concerned, it is an altogether different kind of Specialization and is being dealt in another book named Diploma in Food Production by the same author (Dr Anshumali Pandey).

Furthermore, this book for MT consists of precise and concentrated information which should be used as an arsenal in addition to the regular studies done in the class rooms of the Institute. The hotel chains which rely on this book for seeking questions for elimination rounds are as Taj Group, Oberoi Group, Leela, Lalit Suri Hotels, Park Group, Hilton, ITC Group of Hotels, ITDC, also IRCTC, PVR, INOX, Mc Donalds, and hundreds more,,,,

Congratulations and Best wishes!!

Dr Anshumali Pandey

# CHAPTER ONE

# Career in Food and Beverage Service

### *Preparing for a F&B Career:*

Persons involved in this industry also need to have knowledge about planning and establishing the physical facility for food preparation and service. Some of the personal skills essential to succeed in the food service industry are: An interest in food and regular update of trends in national and international cuisines. Ability to have a good focus on quality, production, sanitation and food cost controls.

Ability to establish, maintain and enforce consistently high performance standards. Good communication and interaction skills (Ability to communicate effectively, both verbally and in writing, to an array of diverse internal and external clients).

Good organising abilities with an eye for detail. Pleasant, cheerful and energetic personality. Good command over English, other preferred languages especially foreign languages. Ability to be on your feet for long hours.

## *Scope:*

Within this one vast industry, there are different kinds of jobs requiring different kinds of skills. Some who have the appropriate training may work in a palatial '7'-star establishment, with a luxurious atmosphere and come into contact with famous and important people of many nationalities. It is an international industry, providing opportunities for trained persons to be able to work abroad for some or throughout their careers.

There is demand for well-trained experienced professionals who can participate in opening hotels and other catering establishments in different countries. Other opportunities to work in this field are in the catering units providing food to cruise ships, airlines and the railways. Large private hospitals also have catering managers in their kitchens, cafeterias and hostels. Most departments in the catering industry are complicated specialisations requiring a great deal of work, dedication, practice and mastery. These are basic qualities that must be possessed by any young person who wants to embark on a career.

### Careers in the Catering and Food Service Industry:

In this industry, a person can work in various positions such as Food Service Supervisor, Cafetaria Manager, Catering Manager, Production Manager, Purchase Manager and Food Service Director /Asst Food Service Director. Placement can be obtained in independent restaurants, corporate restaurants, franchised restaurants, managed services in educational institutions, health care industry, e.g., hospitals, industrial canteens, catering services in travel related transport systems such as air (flight kitchens), trains, cruise lines (ship).

Persons who are interested in cooking, who have good culinary skills, with additional and specialised training can work as Executive Chef, Sous Chef, Chef Tournant, Station Chef. Besides this, there are vast opportunities to take up catering independently. One can set up independent restaurants, corporate restaurants, franchised restaurants.

Also, one can undertake managed services for education, healthcare, business and industry (catering meals at work places), catering in amusement parks, catering in national, state, and regional parks, catering for adventure/eco–tourism, catering for theme parties, product launches, banquets, official functions, etc., preparing and supplying special, nutritionally modified meals/health foods that are low in Calories, fat, and cholesterol, high in fiber and nutrition, breakfast foods that are healthier. Media, particularly television, has stimulated interest in cooking and the different food patterns of various cultures. In fact, the scope of the food service industry is unlimited.

# *Hospitality Industry and the F&B Server*

"A hotel is defined as a place where a valid traveller can receive food and shelter, provided he is in a position to pay for it, and is in a fit condition to be received."

### *Introduction:*

India, a vast country, which has very good potential for the development of Food & Beverage service Industry. The number of people availing the services of food & beverage industry is steadily increasing due to their increased disposable income. Eating out in future will not be a luxury but an essential activity. The food & beverage service industry is different from other industries in satisfying the needs of customers. It satisfies one of the most important physiological needs of the consumer, that is, of hunger and thirst. From last decade food & beverage Industry is expanding very fast.

The F & B department is the send major revenue producing department of the hotel. The Activities of this department are highly complex, demanding varied skills level to perform the job. Waiting at table involves close contact with customers and their food and means that waiters are under constant observation. Food is not appetizing if served by a person who is slovenly and unclean. Uniforms must be clean and well-ironed. A well-trained, smart and helpful staff can sometimes make up for aspects which are lacking elsewhere in the operation. Food & beverage service staff must see that the guest have everything they require and are completely satisfied. It is of great importance to anticipate customers need. Establishment's success depends on effective Co-ordination of all staff; a waiter should aim to help his fellow worker. A co-operative waiter cultivates his ability to get on well with customers and colleagues alike and to further the policies of the Management.

### *History of catering*

The food and beverage service industry in India traces its roots to the traditional community feasts and the movement of people on Pilgrimage thousands of years ago. Most people were on the move primarily for preaching religion and hunting. People took shelter under trees when they were away from their homes and depended on natural sources for their food. Their lives were endangered by wild animals and wayside robbers, which forced them to look for a place that assured them safety, accommodation and food. Dharamshalas and Chatrams came up to protect the lives of travellers from wild animals and robbers. These were buildings where travellers could stay free of cost. The travellers were also provided stables and sheds for horses and bullock carts, respectively, free of charge.

They were given food and accommodation at no cost during the rule of kings. Kings entertained common people and merchants with feasts consisting of a variety of rich dishes, traditional dances, bravery arts, etc, during festivals.

The outsiders who came to India during the course of its history include the Greeks under Alexander the great, the Kushanas from Central Asia, the Mongols under Genghis Khan, Muslim traders and invaders from the Middle East and Central Asia, and finally the British and other Europeans. It was during the Mughal rule that Sarais were developed to provide accommodation to travellers which were later converted to inns and western style hotels during the British rule. The invasion by other dynasties brought in their cultures and cuisines to the land.

Europeans visited the country to trade for the finest cotton textiles as well as spices. Eventually the British colonized the region. They introduced their cuisines, the skills of making wines and distilled drinks and eating habits. Table etiquettes and the art of eating with continue to eat with. However, even today, people continue to eat with their fingers. In Tamil Nadu, people eat their meals from banana leaves and in the north, from a thali. Economic activities Paved the way for development of western-style hotels and restaurants, mainly to cater to the requirements of the British & European traders.

The development of catering in India is mainly attributed to the British, who introduced hotels and restaurants similar to the ones in Europe. The rapid development of transportation, especially the railways in the mid-nineteenth century, enabled people to move in large numbers. This led to the establishment of small lodges and restaurants in and around railway stations to cater to the needs of the travellers. Refreshment rooms at railway stations and Pantry cars in some of the trains were introduced. Reputed hotels such as Taj, The Oberoi and the ambassador were well established when India became independent.

After independence, the hospitality industry grew at a faster rate. Civil aviation developed rapidly soon after the Second World War. The introduction of international flight services in the year 1948 and additional services in the mid-1950s encouraged a lot of foreigners to visit India and also many international chains of hotel such as the Holiday Inn, the Sheraton, and the intercontinental and so on, started their operations in India. The Oberoi group establishment the first franchised hotel with the Inter continental hotels in Delhi in the early 1960s. The people of India, in general did not Prefer dining out till the early 1960s. They always carried with them home made food to the workplace, school a while travelling.

Even today, some people carry food whenever they go out. Perhaps this could be one of the reason for dabbawalas, who are food vendors engaged in distributing meals in dabbas (Boxes) to clients at their workplaces, doing so well in Mumbai. In South India, people used to packed food such as lime rice, tamrind rice and curd rice from vendors. In the north, bhojanalayas served local dishes, especially roti, sabji and salad. Indian Tourism development corporation (ITDC) was set up in 1966 with the developing & expanding tourism infrastructure in the country and thereby promoting India as a tourist destination. ITDC succeeded in achieving its objectives by promoting the largest hotel chain in India and providing all tourist services such as accommodation, catering, transport, in house travel agency and so on. For development of manpower to meet the growing needs of hotels, restaurants and other hospitality based industries.

For this purpose, Institute of Hotel Management (IHM) and Food craft Institute (FCI) were established. These programmes impart adequate knowledge and training in the core operational and managerial areas of the hospitality industry. This makes the students understand the environment and execute their job professionally. In 2002, Ministry of Tourism (MOT) launched a programme called **Capacity Building For service provider** (CBSP) to train persons engaged in small hotels, dhabas, eating joints & and restaurants. Projects Priyadarshini was launched in 2005 to impart training to women in taxi driving/operation, entrepreneurship such as setting up souvenir kiosks and so on, to adopt tourism as their profession. People of different region in India have different style of food like Hyderabadi Cuisine, Avadhi Cuisine, Goan Cuisine, South Indian cuisine etc. A lot of foreign food service organization such as McDonald's, Pizza king, Dominos, subway and soon, have set up their operation in India, which has made local restaurant fine-tune their operations in order to compete with these outlets.

## *Catering establishments:*

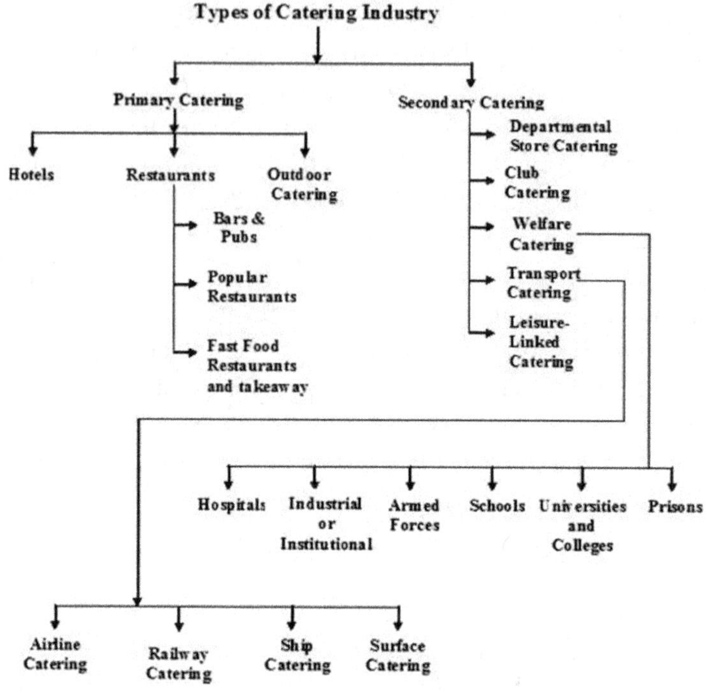


### Primary Catering Establishments:

Establishments such as hotels, restaurants and fast food outlets which are primarily concerned with the provision of food and beverage are called primary catering establishments.

**Hotels:** The main purpose of hotels is to provide accommodation, which may or may not include the service of food & beverage. A hotel may be a small family-run unit providing a limited service in one restaurant, or a large luxury hotel providing service through a number of outlets such as the coffee shop, room service, banquets, specialty restaurant, grill room and cocktail bars. The service in these types of hotels is usually personalized and the tariff is very high, as they generally cater to persons of a high social standing. Medium class hotels are similar to luxury hotels, through their surroundings are less luxurious category. The prices in the various categories of hotels often depend upon the service and choice of food and beverage that they offer to their clientele.

**Restaurant:** The primary function of commercial restaurant is the provision of food & beverage. Restaurants are of different standards. The food service and prices are often comparable to those of similar restaurants in luxury hotels. They offer a wide choice for an elaborate menu and a very high quality of service.

**Bar and Pubs:** The bar serves different types of alcoholic beverages to residential and non-residential guest in the hotel. The idea of pubs is fairly new in India. It has been borrowed from the concept of public houses in English and adapted to Indian conditions. They are geared to provide service of all types of alcohol with an emphasis on draught beer and good music. Food may also be served from a limited menu.

**Popular restaurants:** The objectives of popular catering restaurants are to provide quick and economical meal, in a clean and standardized dining room. These restaurants are commonly used by the vast urban population of India. They are of various styles and categories. Some restaurants serve only vegetarian food while some specialize in the food of a particulars region such as the Punjab or Andhra. Some restaurants serve food from more than one region.

**The entry of pizza parlours** and westernized popular food into India provides the urban Indian a wider choice, in the types of popular restaurants to choose from. The numerous outlets that have sprung up all over the country in the last decade show a new trend in the urban citizen's eating habits. This has resulted in an increased awareness among the public about the availability of various types of cuisine and catering service.

**Fast food restaurants & take away:** There is a predominant American influence in fast food style of catering. The service of food and beverages in a fast food restaurant is at a faster pace, than at an a la carte restaurant as the menu is compiled with a special emphasis on the speed of preparation and service. To make this type of service financially viable, a large turnover of customers is necessary. The investment is rather large, due to the specialized and expensive equipment needed and high labour costs involved.

The take-away or take out service that exploits to the full the concept of —Fast Foods‖. The take away operation offers a limited basic menu to the customer, but within this menu there may be a number of variations on the basic items. The time between customer placing orders and receiving their meals, aims to be faster than any other method of food service. The customer may either take the food out of the take away to eat, or it may be consumed on the premises, a large number of —take-away'outlets now provide seating areas.

**Outdoor / Off-Premise Catering:** This means catering to a large number of people at a venue of their choice. Hostels, restaurants and catering contractors meet this growing demand. The type of food and setup depends entirely on the price agreed upon. Outdoor catering includes catering for functions such as marriages, parties and conventions. Off-premise caterers meet the needs of all markets segments, from the low budget customer who looks for the most quantity and quality for the least amount of money, to the upscale client with an unlimited budget who wants the highest level of service, the ultimate in food quality, and the finest in appointments such as crystal stem ware, silver plated flatware and luxurious linens. Off-premise catering is an art and a science. The art is creating foods and moods, as the caterer and client together turn a vision into reality. The science is the business of measuring money, manpower and material.

### *Secondary Catering Establishments*

In secondary catering industry, the provision of food and beverage is a part of another business such as **welfare catering** and transport catering. Catering establishments are usually classified on the basis of the demands being met by them. The main aim of any catering organization is to attract different sections of the public to use its facilities, keeping in view the price of food and service it offers in relation to the location of the property and the class of clientele it attracts.

**Department store catering:**-Some departmental stores, apart from carrying on their primary activity of retailing their own wares, provide catering as an additional facility. This type of catering evolved when large departmental stores wished to provide food and beverages to their customers as a part of their retailing concept. It is inconvenient and time consuming for customers to take a break from shopping, and have some refreshments at different location. Thus arose the need for some sort of a dining facility in the departmental store itself. This style of catering is becoming more popular and varied nowadays.

**Club Catering:** This refers to the provision of food and beverages and accommodation to a restricted clientele. The origin of this service can be traced back to England, where membership of a club was considered prestigious. Clubs for people with similar interest such as turf club, golf clubs and cricket clubs, to name a few, have sprung up. The service and food in these clubs tend to be of fairly good standards and are economically priced. Facilities provided by the club may include sports, both in-door and outdoor, libraries, swimming pools, social activities, social work, the pursuing a specific hobby etc.

**Welfare catering:** The provision of food and beverages to people to fulfill a social need, determined by a recognized authority, is known as welfare catering. This grew out of the welfare state concept, prevalent in western countries. It include catering in institute or industries, hospitals, schools, colleges, prisons and armed forces.

**Hospital:** Hospital catering facilities have improved considerably over the past years. Hospital catering is a specialized form of catering as the patient is normally unable to move elsewhere and choose alternative facilities and therefore special attention must be given to the food and beverage so that encouragement is given to eat the meal provided. The hospital meals may be considered for the patients, the staff and the general public & visitors. The type of diets required for hospital patients may be classified as full or normal diets, light diets, soft diets, therapeutic diets and special diets.

**Industrial or institutional:** The provision of food and beverage to people at work, in industries and factories at highly subsidized rates is called industrial or institutional catering. It is based on the assumption that **better fed employees are happy and more productive.** Today, labour unions insist on provision of this facility to employees. Catering for a large workforce may be undertaken by the management itself, or may be contracted out to professional caterers. Depending on the choice of the menu suggested by the management, catering contractors undertake to feed the work force for a fixed period of time at a predetermined price.

**Armed forces:** Armed forces, Navy, Army and Air force, the police and fire service and some government departments. The armed forces often have their own specialist catering branches. The levels of food and beverage facilities within the services vary form the large self-service cafeterias for the majority of personnel, to high class traditional restaurants for more senior members of staff. A considerable number of functions are also held by the armed forces leading to both small and large scale banqueting arrangements.

**Schools:** The school meals catering service was formerly structured on a dietary basis with a daily or weekly per capita allowance to ensure that the children obtained edequate nutritional levels from their meals. The school meals service caters for staff and children; in primary schools, children's ages vary from approximately 5 to 11 years and may include some nursery children, and in secondary schools from 12 to 16 or 18 years, Most of the schools used to operate their dining rooms on a family type service or a self-service basis. Nutritional value is important for catering in schools.

**Universities and colleges:** All institutions of further and higher education provide some form of catering facilities for the academic, administrative, technical and secretarial staff as well as for full and part time students and visitors. The catering service in this sector of the industry suffers from an under-utilization of its facilities during the vacation periods and in many instances at the weekends. Universities and colleges are autonomous bodies and are responsible for their own catering services. Residential students pay in advance for their board and lodgings. Non-residential students are provided with an on-site catering provision that has to compete against all other forms of locally provided catering.

**Prisons:** Prisoners are to be catered in prisons. The catering within the prisons is the responsibility of the Jailer with delegated responsibility being given to a catering officer with much of the actual cooking and serving being done by the prisoners themselves. In Tihar Jail, Delhi more than 10,000 prisoners were catered daily three times a day in systematic manner.

**Transport Catering:-** It includes that sector of food and beverage establishment which makes provision of food and beverage of people who are on the move. The provision of food and beverage to passengers, before, during and after a journey on trains, aircrafts, ships and in buses or private vehicles is termed as transport catering. It involves the feeding of a large at a catering facility and who need to be catered for in a specific time, for example, on board a plane.

**Airline Catering:** - Catering to airlines passengers on flights, as well as at restaurants situated at airport is termed as airline catering. Airline catering falls in two main areas:-

**Terminal Catering:** The catering services provided at airport terminals through lounges, cafeterias and takes-away comes under terminal catering.

**In-transit or In-flight catering:** The technological development in the field of aviation has totally revolutionized the catering facilities in air catering. Airlines have to provide food and accommodation to passenger in transit. Whereas passengers are stopped over at the best hotels in the city when they are making a scheduled stop-over at the airlines expenses or when a flight is unduly delayed, thus automatically taking care of the guests comfort. The problems faced by the catering personnel are how to provide delicious and wholesome food to passengers in flight. This is done by preparing all food in flight kitchens on the ground, or getting the food cooked by hotels under contract, freezing it and reheating the food in flight. The reheating of food is now being done by most of the major airlines by the use of microwave ovens in which very high frequency waves heat the food in seconds by inducing very high frequency molecular motion within the food.

The menu for the first class and economy class passengers are different and first class passengers are also served wines free of any additional charge. The food and beverage portions are highly standardized with meal portioned into plastic tray which is presented to passengers and from which they eat their meals. Disposable cutlery, napkins etc are used which reduce the facilities for washing up and cut down on breakage and wastages. For first class passenger garnishing, slicing etc, added according to their request. The crockery used may be bone china with fine glasses and cutlery.

**Railway catering:** Travelling by train for long distances can be very tiring, hence a constant supply of a variety of refreshment choices help to make the Journey less tedious. Catering to railway passengers both during the Journey as well as during halts at different railway station is called railway catering.

**<u>Railway catering may be divided into two Major areas:-</u>**

**Terminal Catering:** Catering at railway terminals usually comprises self-service and waiters service restaurants, fast food and take away units, supplemented by vending machines dispensing hot and cold foods and beverages.

**In-transit catering:** In transit catering can feature three kinds of service:- The first is the traditional restaurant car service where breakfast, lunch and dinner are organized in sitting and passenger go to restaurant car for service where appropriate seating accommodation is provided, and then return to their seats on the train after their meal. The second type of service is the buffet car, which is a self-service operation in which passengers go to the car and buy light refreshments over the counter. The third is a trolley service where snacks and drinks are delivered to customer at their seats. Pantry car is attached with passenger trains for production of food.

**Ship Catering:** voyages by sea were once a very popular mode of travelling, but with the onset of air travel, sea voyages have declined sharply. However, recently, it has again become popular with a large number of people opting for pleasure cruises. Both cargo and passenger ship have kitchens and restaurants on board. The quality of food, service and facilities offered depends on the class of the ship and the price the passengers are wiling to pay. There are cruises to suit every pocket. There are cruises of two to five days duration which offer budget accommodation comparable to a limited service hotel, while luxury cruises of seven days to three months duration offer luxurious staterooms and various other facilities that are comparable a first class resort. Luxury cruises pamper travellers with deluxe accommodation and attentive and specialized service at a very high premium. All these ships provide a variety of food and beverage service outlets, to cater to the individual needs of the passengers. They range from room service and cocktail bars to specialty dining restaurants. The ships that cater to the cruise sector today, are virtually flouting palaces with every conceivable guest service available abroad them. This sector has been growing in popularity in recent times, and has become affordable to a large cross section of people. Cruise companies offer attractive packages to passenger.

**Surface catering:** surface catering has progressed from the inns and taverns of earlier days used by those travelling on foot and horse back to the present day motorway service areas and other roadside catering outlets. Catering to passengers travelling by surface transport such as buses and private vehicles is called surface catering. These eating establishments are normally located around a bus terminus or on highways catering service to the traveling public and their food and beverage facilities usually include self-service and waiter service restaurants, vending machines and take-away foods and beverages.

**Leisure-linked catering:** This type of catering refers to the provision of food and beverages to people engaged in leisure. The increase in leisure and a large disposable income for leisure activities has made it a very profitable form of catering. This includes the provision of food and beverage through different stalls and kiosks at exhibitions, theme parks, galleries and theatres.

## *What F&B professionals do differently?*

### <u>While Talking to a Guest</u>

- Always smile while welcoming the guest in your restaurant.
- Always maintain an interested and helpful expression on your face.
- Maintain eye contact. Even if you are busy writing or serving, look up once in a while to maintain eye contact.

- Maintain a distance of at least two feel from the guest while taking an order.
- Speak softly and clearly, without artificial accent.
- Avoid unnecessary movements of hands and facial gestures while describing dishes, or while speaking to guests.

## While standing

- While standing to take an order or standing at the restaurant door, stand erect at ease, but not in a casual manner.
- Weight balanced
- Shoulders straight
- Chest out
- Stomach in
- Keep your hands on the sides or behind your back.
- Do not keep your hands in the pockets or on the hips.
- Do not cross your arms across the chest.
- Do not lean against the sideboard, panels or the reservation desk/Maitre D's desk.
- Remember, you may be in view of a guest even when you are not directly interacting with him/her. Maintain your poise at all times.
- Do not huddle together in bunches inside the restaurant. There is always something to be done in your area, even when the guests are not there.

## While walking

- Walk at an even pace inside the restaurant, avoiding any sound of the footsteps.
- Never run inside the restaurant
- While walking in guest area. If guest are approaching, get aside and give them
- First right of way.
- If near a door, open the door for the guests to pass through
- Walk on the left hand side
- If accompanying a guest, walk on his/her right hand side and open the door for the guest.
- Walk erect and maintain the poise

## While talking to colleagues

- While communicating with your colleagues, do not point your finger towards any guest. Use cover numbers to describe who has ordered for what.
- Do not use abusive language with your colleagues.
- Speak politely while ordering food. Calling for pick up etc.
- Be aware of your conversation over the phone. Guest may be watching, or hearing.
- Never shout in to the telephone
- Do not have long conversations on phone, while a guest is waiting.
- Do not entertain personal calls while at work.

## Courteous Behaviour

- Anticipate guest needs and fulfil them without being asked. For example:
- Open the restaurant door and let the guest pass ahead.
- Hand him a pen as he reaches for his own.
- Light his cigarette, as he gets ready to light it.
- Reach out for the heavy bag he is carrying.
- Do not get familiar with the guest, even when he treats when he treats you like a
- Friend. Maintain professional relationship.
- Treating guest courteously and turning to a colleague and talking to him impolitely destroy the image. Maintain the same finesse and politeness.
- Treat non resident guest with as much respect as resident guest.
- They are potential guests too.
- Do not forget the power of _word of mouth publicity' that the guests do for your restaurant.

## Physical Attributes:

The physical attributes contains the proper personal hygiene and appearance. Since waiting staff deals with food, utmost cleanliness and good grooming is necessary at all times. This applies not only in high class hotels, but in every branch of catering however humble it may be. Guest is not likely to return to an establishment where staff does not maintain proper hygiene and grooming. There are times when food & beverage professionals are required to work overtime. Lifting and carrying service equipment also requires staff to be physically fit.

**Hair:** Hair should be kept healthy, trimmed and avoid dandruff. Hair should never fall over the eyes. Waitresses may adopt neat hair styles and particularly ensure a hair length which does not fall on to or below the collar or lengthy hair should be combed and tied neatly and properly.

**Bath:** Bath every day, without fail, before coming to shift.

**Face:** - Males should shave every day, before coming to shift. Moustache, if kept must be neatly trimmed. Do not use strong aftershave. Ladies should wear only light make-up. Do not use heavy perfumes.

**Teeth:** Teeth and a clean mouth are vital, both for appearance and a wholesome breath. Brush your teeth immediately before coming to duty. Do not eat onion, garlic or smoke before your shift. If you smoke, use mouthwash.

**Hands:** Always wash hands with soap before coming on shift keep your nails short and clean. Hands must always be clean, free of any stains and skin breaks. Always wash hands with soap, immediately after using toilets, cating, smoking or handling refuse.

**Uniform:** Uniform should always be clean, laundered and ironed. Change uniform whenever it is visibly soiled. Change socks and undergarments everyday. Always carry a handkerchief and change it daily. Uniform must be worm only on duty and not for personal use.

**Feet:** Feet need care, both for comfort and cleanliness. Keep toe nails trim and feet well washed. Corns and other painful blemishes may require treatment by a chiropodist disease. For more severe foot weakness medical advice should be sought. Socks or stockings should be changed and washed daily.

**Shoes:** Wear comfortable closed toed shoes. Air your shoes. Waitresses should avoid excessively high and pointed heels and shoes should be daily polished.

**Cuts and burns:** cuts and burns must be covered with correct dressing.

**Illness:** Inform your supervisor, if you suffer from:-

- Fever
- Diarrhoea
- Upset stomach, nausea or vomiting
- Sore throat or sinus infection
- Coughing or sneezing
- Conjunctivitis

It is better to have regular hours of sleep under good conditions rather than long irregular hours of sleep. Exercise is very essential for normal growth and development of the body and the perfect maintenance of health.

**Posture:** Good stance is also important for the appearance comfort and efficiency of waiting staff. To stand upright and walk erect is to give a good impression to guests and also to avoid the bodily stresses that accompany slouching. Waitresses who require support garments are advised to choose sound quality and proper fitting ones to aid posture and health as well as comfort and appearance.

## *Inter and intra departmental co-operation:*

The food and beverage service department is the selling point of the Hotel. In order to enable maximum and efficient selling, other departments in a hotel also play important roles. It requires a working knowledge of other departments and their functioning to achieve this.

**Food Production:** In a service outlet, the F& B production has the most important role to play. Items prepares here are the ones that the service person sell. In the planning has any Restaurant, the first thing that comes to mind is the menu.

**Kitchen Stewarding:** This department is involved in the general cleanliness and upkeep of the kitchen. It has a pot wash where large vessels are cleaned and a wash area where service equipment is cleaned, washed and stored .This department also deals with the shortage and issue all service and kitchen equipment and hence the controls are also part of this department. The kitchen stewarding departments is headed a chief executive steward or steward manager. The requisitions of the service equipment are done through a kitchen stewarding indent book with signature from the outlet manager, F&B Manager and chief Executive steward.

**Accounts:** The service department does not deal with the Accounts department directly but indirectly through various outlet cashiers. The cashiers receive the copy of the KOT and raise bill accordingly. They also have detailed information about credit card and discount policies, etc. The general account department deals with payments of the company like employee salaries, bill settlements, vouchers etc. On a day – to- day level, the dining room is in direct coordination with the cashiers, and on a weekly basis with the control of KOT books and discrepancies with regard to entries in the KOT, bill authorization of signature etc.

**House Keeping:** The House keeping department takes care of general upkeep of the Hotel. It undertakes periodic cleaning of all public areas including cleaning of carpet and polishing of fittings. Service personnel may call on housekeeping staff to take care of occasional spillage, accidents etc. In the event of a guest's clothes getting spoilt, the house keeping staff will assist in laundering them, thus helping retain the customer. This department also organizes to have flower arrangements placed in the hotel . The book used in connection with housekeeping is the linen book, which lists all service linen used and exchanged on a **"One to One basis"** of the more costly items in the overheads.

**Engineering:** This department takes care of the air- Conditioning, lighting, plumbing and general maintenance. Communication is done through the maintenance work order book and reminders are used if required. Good coordination with the department is vital for the upkeep of equipment and helps to prevent breakdown during service.

**Front Office:** This is a **"Front of the - house"** position and deals with the guest directly. The check –in, check-out, billing, information, reservation, bell desk, telephones etc. all come under this department. The front office department may also be in- charge of the health club, beauty parlour, business centre and travel desk. All communication relating to the status of a guest (VIP, HG), group staying, company guests etc can be obtained from the front office. The dining room and room service need to coordinate with the front office for guest lists, billing instructions, amenities placement in rooms, problem handling during the night shift and other allied service.

**Stores:** This may be one or divided into separate areas such as food, liquor, materials, perishables etc. It may get its supplies through the purchase department gives the stores department its requirements of food items like proprietary sauces and seasonings and materials like doilies, paper napkins, candles, office materials, etc. through the corresponding indent book.

**Personnel Department:** All areas of staff requirement and employment are dealt by the personnel department in collusion with the concerned heads of departments **(HODs).** Any action to be taken regarding discipline will also be dealt with in the same way. This department is also in charge of the staff cafeteria, lockers etc. The service personnel get their leave applications processed and leave cards updated by the personnel department. This department also handles discrepancies in the time card. Job descriptions and job specifications are drawn up by this department in accordance with requirements from the individual departments. Recruitment, induction, training, evaluation and personality development programmes are also conducted by this department in the absence of a separate training cell.

**Security:-**This department handles the safety aspect of the organization. It is required to conduct safety and first aid drills, and fire fighting exercises. Security personnel also look into vehicle parking and are in close contact with the local police to look out for known criminals and Anti-social elements. Service personnel may use security personnel in case of drunks and unpaid bills. They have to maintain law and order in the establishment it and when difficult situations occur.

# *Food and Beverage Service Glossary Terms:*

- **A la Carte** – The menu in which all the items are individually priced and customer select and combined dishes according to their choice
- **Aboyeur:** The person in a traditional kitchen brigade who controls the hotplate and is responsible for communication between kitchen and waiting staff and who Calls up the orders. Barker.
- **Aerated Drinks:** Drinks which contain carbon-dioxide either naturally or to which $CO_2$ is introduced to cause aeration.
- **Agenda:** A list of speakers, presentations and associated timings, given to conference delegates as part of the pre-registration or on-site registration.
- **Aging:** Wine is aged in bottles and the period of aging may differ from house to house for example Bordeaux and Burgundy wines are aged for 3-4 years while Chablis is aged for 18 months.
- **Air Conditioning, Comfort.** Use of air conditioning solely for human comfort, as compared with conditioning for industrial processes or manufacturing.
- **Air Conditioning, Industrial.** Use of air conditioning in industrial plants where the prime objective is enhancement of a manufacturing process

rather than human comfort.

- **Air Conditioning.** The process of altering air supplies to control simultaneously its humidity, temperature, cleanliness, and distribution to meet specific criteria for a space. Air conditioning may either increase or decrease the space temperature.
- **Alcohol Free Wines:** Alcohol free wines are also known as de-alcoholized wine or non alcoholic wine. These wines start out as real fermented wine, but before it is bottled, it is either filtered or put through a spinning process that removes both the water and the alcohol. Ales (Top fermented beer): Ale is a strong beer that was originally popular in the United Kingdom.
- **Ales:** are more aromatic and have more pronounced flavour, alcoholic content ranging from 4-5%. Ale is top fermented when the yeast has finished its job, its rises to the top of the liquid rather than settling at the bottom. Ale normally requires less aging than lagar does and can sold within a days after its fermentation is completed. Different types of ales arc following:
- **American Breakfast:** According to Buinessdictionary.com, American breakfast is, A hotel breakfast that includes most or all of the following: two eggs (fried or poached), sliced bacon or sausages, sliced bread or toast with jam/jelly/butter, pancakes with syrup, cornflakes or other cereal, coffee/tea, orange/grapefruit juice'. Coffee is most preferred beverage in American breakfast.
- **American Scale:** It is used in United States and in this system 50% alcohol is equal to 100° therefore 100% alcohol is equal to 200° proof.
- **American Whiskey:** The Americans spell whisky as 'whiskey'. All American Whiskies are made from cereal (generally, a mixture of various grains of cereals), distilled mostly in patent still at no more than 90% and aged in oak barrels (except for corn whiskey which may not be aged) and bottled at not less than 40% A.B.V. The following are the types of whiskey from the U.S.A
- **Añejo (Aged):** It is aged for minimum period of one year, but less than three years in government controlled oak casks, which add colour and mellow the spirit.
- **Annual Operating Budget:** The formal business and financial plan for a business for one year.
- annual) estimate of an organization's revenue and expenditure; amount of money needed

- **AOC (Appellation d'OrigineControlée)** : Controlled Designation of Origin, equivalent of AVA (American Viticultural Area) in the States. This classification acts as a consumer guarantee that a wine is of a particular quality and generally of a particular style.
- **AOP (Appellation d'Origine Protegée)** : the European equivalent of the French AOC.
- **Armagnac:** Armagnac is the world's second best brandy produced in the Armagnac region of France from the Department of 'Gers', south-east of Bordeaux. The main grape varieties used in production of Armagnac are Saint -Émillion (elsewhere Ugni Blanc), Folle Blanche, Colombard and Baco Blanc.
- **Aromatized Wine:** Aromatized wine is a fortified wine in which herbs, roots, flowers, barks and other flavouring agents have been steeped in order to change the natural flavours of the wine.
- **Attendance:** The overall total number of people at an event.
- **Audio-visual:** Has both a sound and visual component. Typically in the form of images and recorded speech or music.
- **Auguste Escoffier:** The most famous French chef, known as the emperor of chefs.
- **Award Ceremony:** An event where the performance of individuals and groups in a company or industry are recognised. It is use to honour and motivate key staff.
- **Back bar:** it is located behind the front bar leaving adequate space for the bar tenders to work. It holds all kinds of alcoholic beverages in an attractive manner. Few equipments like storage cabinets, bottle cooler, etc are located in the back bar.
- **Bagasse:** The residue of sugarcane is called a bagasse.
- **Baize base cloth:** Soft felt cloth usually green in colour used on most dining tables in restaurants and banquets.
- **Baize:** It is a thick woollen material which is used to cover the wooden table tops to reduce noise and to hold the tableware at its place.
- **Banquet Service** – It involves serving a meal to a group of people who are celebrating, gathering for a special occasion like conference, meetings etc.
- **Banquet:** It is a formal meal followed by speeches. However in the hotel industry it means all kinds of function catering.
- **Bar die:** It is the vertical structure supporting the top of the front bar which separates the customer's side from the bartender's work area.

- **Bar:** a licensed retail business establishment that serves alcoholic beverages, such as beer, wine, liquor, cocktails, and other non alcoholic beverages along with snacks or full restaurant menu for consumption on premises.
- **Barley Wine:** Barley wine is style of strong ale of between 8-12% alcohols by volume. This beer is sweet and strong and sold in small bottles or nips.
- **Beverage Cost:** It refers to the cost of beverages sold.
- **Bin Card:** It is a storeroom card for each drink with bin number showing stock in hand, maximum stock level, minimum stock level and reorder level of the stock.
- **Binder:** The binder is the leaf in which the filler is wrapped to form what is known as cigar bunch (Filler and binder together is called "bunch")
- **Binning:** The wines should be laid down horizontally so that the cork is always in contact with wine and so does not dry out.
- **Bitter Rot:** Bitter rot is fungal disease of ripens grapes that are active in warm, humid conditions. It is found on damaged tissues and the bitter fruit flavour can be detected in the finished wine.
- **Black Rot:** Black Rot is a fungal disease which is one of the most economically important diseases of vines in the north eastern U.S, Canada and parts of Europe and South America.
- **Blanc:** White.
- **Blanco (White):** It is tequila without aging and it is very clear, without any colour. Some blancos are kept for a little time in wax lined oak or stainless steel containers, which reduce the harshness that is very common with blancos. They are also called plata (Silver).
- **Blending:** This is an art that requires considerable experience, judgment and sensibility. It is a legitimate, natural and honest way of improving the quality of wine.
- **Blind receiving:** In this there is no invoice accompanying the delivery of items from the supplier. Invoice is generated at the stores itself while receiving the supplies.
- **Blush Wine:** It is a new style of rosé wine developed in California. Skins of black grapes are allowed to macerate with the must for a very short period which produces a very light pink colour wine. Red and white grapes are used together.
- **Bock Beer:** Bock is a strong lager of German origin. Different sub styles exist including Maibock, Doppelbock etc.

- **Body Language** - Body language refers to any kind of bodily movement or posture, including facial expression, which transmits a message to the observer. In other words it represents the gestures, postures, and facial expressions by which a person manifests various physical, mental, or emotional states and communicates nonverbally with others.
- **BOT:** Bar Order Ticket
- **Bottled Cider:** It is a pasteurized and filtered cider bottle with dosages of yeast and sugar to induce secondary fermentation in the bottle. Secondary fermentation can be done in closed tanks or impregnated with carbon dioxide gas. This drink has effervescence and termed as pomagne (produced by Bulmers in the U.K). Bottled ciders are marketed as vintage or special.
- **Bottling:** Spirit is added to liqueur to bring it to the correct alcoholic strength, if necessary. All liqueurs are given a final filtration to ensure star bright clarity before bottling.
- **Bottling:** The wine is subsequently bottled in clean and sterilized bottles.
- **Break-even Point:** It is the level of sales where there is no profit or loss. It is a point where total sales equals total expense or the point where total contribution equals fixed expenses.
- **Breakfast dishes** includes bread (plain/toasted), egg (boiled, poached, scrambled, omelette, etc.), porridge, cornflakes, fish, meat and poultry and beverages like tea, coffee, milk, hot chocolate and canned/fresh juices of fruits and vegetables.
- **Breakfast:** According to Oxford Advanced Learners Dictionary, breakfast means –the first meal of the day. It is very important meal of the day.
- **Briefing:** two way communication between management and staff before an operation
- **Brigade:** The staff in the dining room or kitchen as an organized team.
- **British Thermal Unit (Btu):** Quantity of heat required to raise the temperature of 1 lb of water 1_F at or near 39.2_F, which is its temperature of maximum density.
- **Brunch Buffet:** It consists of both breakfast and lunch menu items. While this leaves caterers with many menu items from which to choose, it's better to serve lighter items than more filling ones.
- **Brut:** Dry.
- **Budget:** It is a comprehensive plan in writing, stated in monetary terms, that outline the expected financial consequences of management's plans

and strategies for accomplishing the organization's mission for the coming period.

- **Budgetary control:** It refers to any management approach that involves setting some kind of targets, regularly measuring variances between the original targets and actual outcomes, and motivating people to reduce those variances.
- **Budgeting:** An estimate of revenue or income and expenditure made by a company/ unit /hotel
- **Buffet:** Meal consisting of a number of dishes set out so that guest can select what they want for themselves.
- **Butler/valet:** A highly trained member of the staff who takes care of all the needs of a resident guest.
- **Café complet:** The term _café complet' is widely used in continental Europe and means a continental breakfast with coffee as the beverage. The term **thé complet'** is also used, with tea provided as the beverage.
- **Café simple or thé simple:** Café simple or thé simple is just a beverage (coffee or tea) with nothing to eat.
- **Call:** Spirits used when patrons do name— or —call—a specific spirit brand in a drink order. (Example: Tanqueray and tonic.) Call bottles tend to be your more popular brands, but are generally not the most expensive.
- **Calorific Value of Fuel:** The calorific value of a fuel is amount of heat liberated by its complete combustion.
- **Captain:** A supervisor of service staff in the food and beverage service department.
- **Carbonated:** A liquid to which CO2 is introduced in order to create a fizz.
- **Carhops:** Waiters working in the drive- in outlets who takes order and deliver the food to the guest.
- **Carousel** – It is rotating shelve (usually three) at different heights containing food, where the guest remains standing, taking his choice of meal from the revolving carouse land placing it on his tray
- **Cash bar:** All the guests pay the bartender for their drinks. In some cases, drink vouchers can be purchased at a centralized location, which makes it easier on the bartenders and controls the collection of money.
- **Catering:** Providing the service of food & beverage.
- **Cave:** Wine cellar.
- **Cellar:** It is a storage space for alcoholic drinks.

- **Cellaring and Second Pressing**: Once the fermentation is complete the "Running Wine" or "VIN DE GOUTTE" is run off into cask for maturing.
- **Central Heating or Cooling Plant**: One large heating or cooling unit used to heat or cool many rooms, spaces, or zones or several buildings, as compared to individual room, zone, or building units.
- **Cépage** : Varietal / Grape.
- **Chafing dish**: A food warmer used during buffet service.
- **Chaptalization / Sugaring**: in case of insufficient alcoholic potential of the MUST, cane sugar is added to improve the alcoholic potential. The process of addition of cane sugar to the MUST to improve the alcohol potential is called CHAPTALIZATION, in Germany it is legal.
- **Château** : Estate. Literally castle, but mostly refers to large country houses.
- **Cider:** Cider is an alcoholic beverage made from the fermented juice of cider apples. It is also legally permitted to make cider from the mixture of apple juice and pear juice in proportion of 75:25 respectively. Although cider can be made from any variety of apples, certain cultivars are known as Ciders apple, which have perfect sugar, acid and tannin content to produce cider.
- **Client:** The person or party that hires an event planner and/or various event components required to hold the event.
- **Coaster:** A small mat Put under a bottle or glass to avoid wet rings on the surface of the table.
- **Coefficient of Performance:** For machinery and heat pumps, the ratio of the effect produced to the total power of electrical input consumed.
- **Coffee Shop:** It is a restaurant open round the clock, providing a multi cuisine menu.
- **Cognac:** It is produce in the Cognac region of France in the department of Charente and Charente-Maritime and considered most famous and prestigious. Brandy produced from grapes grown in the vineyards of the delimited district of Cognac, surrounding the ancient town of Cognac, on the Charente River. Modern delimitation done in 1909, a decree was made to protect Cognac from intimation and accordingly to get Cognac name, the spirit must be made entirely from grapes grown in the delimited region.
- **Colour rendering index:** A numerical scale from 0 to 100 that indicates how bright a colour appears based on how much light is shining on it.

- **Combined Settlement Method:** A guest may elect to use more than one settlement method to bring the folio balance to zero.
- **Comfort Zone:** An area plotted on a psychometric chart to indicate a combination of temperatures and humidifies at which, in controlled tests, more than 50% of the persons were comfortable.
- **Concept:** The idea for a restaurant, which encompasses menu, theme, décor and other factors that create an image in the minds of customers.
- **Concert:** A public performance of music (singer(s) and/or instrumentalist(s)) with entertainment purposes. Concerts could have various forms: indoor or outdoor, paid or free, for-profit or fundraising/ cause events.
- **Condensate:** Liquid formed by the condensation of steam or water vapour.
- **Condensers:** Special equipment used in air conditioning to liquefy a gas.
- **Condensing Unit:** A complete refrigerating system in one assembly, including the refrigerant compressor, motor, condenser, receiver, and other necessary accessories.
- **Conduction, Thermal.** A process in which heat energy is transferred through matter by transmission of kinetic energy from particle to particle, the heat flowing from hot points to cooler ones.
- **Conference:** discussion about a specific matter, mainly organized by a learned society, and based on a precise agenda. The conference has a didactic goal but can also be the opportunity to exchange knowledge with the participants. It is often organized on the occasion of a congress or a symposium
- **Consolidated Hotel Budget:** The summary budget for the entire hotel including revenues, expenses, and profit.
- **Continental Breakfast:** According to Buinessdictionary.com, _A hotel breakfast that may include sliced bread with butter/jam/honey, cheese, meat, croissants, pastries, rolls, fruit juice and various hot beverages.
- **Contribution Margin Ratio:** It is a contribution margin as a percentage of total sales.
- **Control Cycle:** A continuous cycle process of food purchasing, receiving, storing, issuing, preparation, again storing, serving/selling and accounting is said to be a control cycle.
- **Controlling:** Controlling is a process by which the management ensures that the plans and objectives laid down are as per the schedule and the target set would be achievable.

- **Cooling Effect, Total:** The difference in total heat in an airstream entering and leaving a refrigerant evaporator or cooling coil.
- **Cooling Tower:** A mechanical device used to cool water by evaporation in the outside air. Towers may be atmospheric or induced- or powered-draft type.
- **Cooling Unit, Self-Contained:** A complete air-conditioning assembly consisting of a compressor, evaporator, condenser, fan motor, and air filter ready for plugging to an electric power supply.
- **Cooling, Evaporative:** Cooling effect produced by evaporation of water, the required heat for the process being taken from the air. (This method is widely used in dry climates with low wet-bulb temperatures.)
- **Cooling, Sensible:** Cooling of a unit volume of air by a reduction in temperature only.
- **Cooling:** A heat-removal process usually accomplished with air-conditioning equipment.
- **Coopérative :** A cooperative or more likely, a syndicate of wine growers.
- **Corking:** The bottles are finally corked and sealed with Spanish wax. Corks are made from bark of tree called „QUERCUS SUBER" and the best corks are produced in Portugal.
- **Cost:** The amount of expenditure incurred on or attributable to a given thing.
- **Cost-Volume Profit:** It is the relationship between an organization's revenue, costs and the level of activity presented in a graphic form.
- **Côte/Coteaux :** Slope of a hill/hillsides.
- **Cover -** The space required on a table for laying cutlery, crockery, glassware and liner for one person to partake of a meal.
- **Crémant:** A style of sparkling wine other than Champagne.
- **Crockery:** Crockery or chinaware is made up of silica, soda ash, & china clay, & dry glazed to give its a fine finish. It is available in different design & colour. It is more heat resistant to glassware. These are available in different types like – bone china, earthenware, stoneware & porcelain.
- **Cru:** Growth, denotes status of a winery or vineyard.
- **Crushing/Pressing:** The grapes are crushed or pressed according to the local tradition and custom either by feet or more conveniently by mechanical pressure to extract the juice called "MUST".
- **Cultural Event:** An event related to and honouring culture in its various forms and aspects and considered as valuable, enriching and enlightening for the society.

- **Cutlery:** The term cutlery denotes all forms of knives & other cutting equipments. Like – fish knife, butter knife, gateaux slicer, etc.
- **Cuvéespéciale** : Special blend or batch, AKA —reserve wineǁ. Term derived from the French word *"cuve"*, meaning vat or tank. Generally indicates a higher quality wine.
- **Dark Rum:** It has a strong and pungent flavour. It is aged for a longer duration (six years) in charred oak cask. It gets its dark brown colour from wood, caramel, and/or residual molasses. This rum is extensively used in cookery especially in the preparation of cakes, sweets and ice cream.
- **Decaffeinated Coffee:** Coffee from which most of the caffeine has been extracted by processing the green beans under steam in vacuum.
- **Degorgement:** Process of clearing the wine by freezing the segments.
- **Dehumidification:** In air conditioning, the removal of water vapor from supply air by condensation of water vapor on the cold surface of a cooling coil.
- **Delegate:** To entrust a task to another person.
- **Demi sec:** Medium dry.
- **Design:** In a space plan, the definition of sizes, shapes, styles and decoration of facility and furnishings.
- **Destalking or removal of stalks:** The stalks are removed from the grapes by a destalking machine. Destalking is necessary if white wine is made but not if red wine is made.
- **Dhaba:** It is a roadside food stall located at national and state highway specialize in tandoori and Punjab style of cooking.
- **Dog:** A menu engineering classification of items which are neither profitable nor popular.
- **Domaine:** Estate.
- **Doux:** Sweet.
- **Downward Communication:** Downward communication is the information that is exchanged between a manager and a subordinate in other words from top level to low level.
- **Draught Cider:** This is usually unfiltered and has a dosage of yeast and sugar to induce fermentation which gives sparkle to the product and termed as cask conditioned cider. It is slightly sweet with sparkle. If it is complete dry, it is known as scrumpy or farmhouse cider. It is marketed in oak casks or plastic containers.

- **Dry Wines:** Dry wines produced by grapes with less sugar content and the fermentation is allowed to continue till all the sugar is almost or fully consumed.
- **Duplicate Method:** in this method the order is taken in two copies. The top copy goes to the supply point, second copy is retained for service and billing purposes.
- **Duty roaster:** It is a list or plan showing turns of duty or leave in an organization. Having a duty roster not only helps keep your staff organized and minimizes the amount of time spent on hotel chores but also makes a measurable difference in work done by different staff.
- **Egg to Order:** Egg is one of the most versatile items that are served in breakfast. The egg may be served as hard boiled, poached, scrambled, fried, baked, omelette etc.
- **English Breakfast:** English breakfast is heavy and includes variety of dishes like fruit juices, stewed fruits, breakfast cereals, egg to order, fish, meat, bread with butter/preserves and beverages like coffee, tea, hot chocolate etc.
- **Entertainment:** A show or performance designed to amuse and entertain an audience.
- **Evaporator:** A cooling coil in a refrigeration system in which the refrigerant is evaporated and absorbs heat from the surrounding fluid (airstream).
- **Event communication:** refers to a non-media communication tool, which can be internal or external, used by companies or institutions with the intention of organizing an event, generally in the form of a trade fair, a congress, an incentive, a gala dinner etc... This event is thought and realized by a specialized agency, comparable to an advertising agency.
- **Event Manager:** A person in charge of planning, organising, and executing all types and sizes of events.
- **Event Planner:** A person who coordinates all aspects of professional meetings and events.
- **Extra Añejo (Extra Aged):** It is aged for a minimum period of three years in oak casks.
- **Fair:** A public, live event gathering people for a variety of entertainment or commercial activities. It could last from one afternoon to several weeks.
- **Feedback:** The process of sharing thoughts and observations – can be positive or negative.

- **Fermentation**: Fermentation is the action of the yeast on the sugar (grape juice) to convert it into alcohol and carbon dioxide. Yeast cells excrete enzymes that convert natural fruit sugars into almost equal quantities of alcohol and carbonic gas.
- **Filler**: (Shredded Tobacco): The filler is the inner core that forms the body and the shape of cigar.
- **Filtering**: The wine is then passed through wine filters and filtered several times to produce a clear star-bright wine.
- **Fine Champagne** – It is the blend of brandies produced from grapes grown in Grande Champagne (minimum 50%) and Petit Champagne areas
- **Finger bowl**: Small bowl filled with water and perhaps a piece of lemon placed on the table so that guests can clean their finger.
- **Fining**: This is process of clarifying the young wine during its stay in the cask and is done by adding various fining agents (such as Isinglass, Egg White, Bentinite and Gelatin etc.) to the wine which cause wine to coagulate and settle in the bottom of the cask. After fining the wine is racked once again.
- **Fixed Cost**: The cost which remains fixed irrespective to quantum of output over a certain capacity of the organization
- **Flambé**: To pour alcohol over food and set it alights, to enhance visual delight during service.
- **Flatware**: It consists of all forms of spoons and forks.
- **Flavoured Rum**: This rum is flavoured with fruits such as orange, lime, apricot, plums, banana, coconut etc.
- **Flavoured Vodka**: It is flavoured with various spices, herbs, and fruits, e.g. Absolut – Citron, Mandrin, Pepper, Apeach, and Vanilla.
- **Flowering**: The most critical period of a vine's life is when it flowers. At this stage frost, hail, rain, wind and extreme temperatures could wipe out a crop before the growing season begins in earnest.
- **Food service**: Food service is an operation in which products/services are created and delivered to the customer almost simultaneously.
- **Forecasting**: It is an approximation, prediction, or projection of food & beverage sales based on past record and/or information available at the time, with the recognition that other pertinent facts are unclear or unknown.
- **Formal buying**: In this method quotations are invited from suppliers for items against fixed specification. The request for bids may be made

through news papers or any other media. All the quotations are received sealed, and are opened on a said day when it is made final.

- **Formal Communication Network:** A formal communication network is one which is created by management and described with the help of an organizational chart.

- **Fortified Wines:** These are the wines which are fortified with spirit like brandy during vinification when fermentation process is going on. If fortification is done in the beginning of fermentation the end product is sweet fortified wine. If fortification is towards the end of fermentation, the resultant wine is dry fortified wine.

- **Fraud:** It is an act by employees may lead to a reduction in revenue levels and increase in F & B cost percentage.

- **French toast:** in different versions is popular in many regions, and it has the advantage of being an excellent way to utilize day-old bread. Basic French toast consists of slices of bread dipped in a batter of eggs, milk, a little sugar, and flavourings. French toast is cooked on a griddle like pancakes. Variations may be created by changing the basic ingredients.

- **Front bar:** This is the portion of the bar where the customers place their order and receive it. This is actually the interaction point of a customer and the bar tender.

- **Front of House:** The front of house is a term given to the public area of the catering premise or the actual dining room itself. People, who works in this area are called front of house staff including, wait staff, bar staff etc.

- **Fruit Beers & Flavoured Beers:** Variety of beers with additional flavouring such as honeydew or fruit beers, which have fresh fruits such as raspberry or strawberry introduced during the making process to add flavour.

- **Fuel:** A fuel is a substance which when once raised to its ignition temperature continues to burn if sufficient oxygen or air is available.

- **Full Bodied Wine:** These wines have heavy body, texture and higher alcoholic content, rich taste with forceful flavour.

- **Gangway:** It is the free space available between the chairs and the tables which allows the people to move freely.

- **Gay Lussac (GL) scale:** It is used in France and in the most of Europe. The absolute is rated as 100; hence proof is equal to the percentage of alcohol in the spirit. So if whisky has 42% alcohol it is 42° proof GL.

- **Generic Wines**: Generic wines are those wines which are named after the long established European areas. Many North American and Australian wines are labelled as Claret, Burgundy, Chablis, Graves, Hock and even Champagne.
- **Glass rail:** It is a 3 inch width rail running along the bar tender's side for keeping the prepared drink glasses.
- **Glassware:** Glassware is a collective term for various types of glasses which mainly found in bar section. There are various types of glassware of different shapes and sizes, all serving their own purpose. Learning which drinks belong to which glass is beneficiary to both you and your customers.
- **Goal:** A specific intended result of a strategy; often used interchangeably with Objective.
- **Gold Rum:** It obtains its colour either while maturing in charred oak casks or from the small quantity of caramel. It is normally aged for three years. It has more flavour than white Rum.
- **Gold:** It is cask matured to get gold colour. Vodka is matured in the wooden cask to derive olden colour from the wood.
- **Grading:** After harvesting the grapes are taken to winery where they are graded as per specification. In the winery the rotten & unnecessary grapes are separated from the good ones.
- **Grand cru:** Great growth. Highest possible classification for a French wine.
- **Grande Champagne / Grande Fine Champagne–** It is the cognac produced entirely from brandies, made from the grapes grown in Grande Champagne region.
- **Grappe:** Cluster.
- **Green Wines:** It is a Portuguese wine comes from vine grown on the granitic soil in the province of Minho. These are acid wines of low alcoholic content, white, rosé and red wines are made.
- **Grey Rot:** Grey Rot sometimes known as grey mould and one of the most harmful of the fungal diseases that attacks vines. In this form of rot the Botrytis Cinera fungus rapidly spreads throughout the berry flesh and skins breaks down.
- **Grooming:** Good Grooming is commonly used to refer to a person's appearance. It is made up of personal hygiene, tidy hair, appropriate dressing for an occasion.

- **Gross profit or kitchen profit:** the excess of sales over the cost of food expressed as a percentage, or in financial terms.
- **Gueridon:** A Gueridon is a movable service table or trolley on which food may be carved, filleted, flambé or prepared and served to the guest according to his/ her choice.
- **HACCP:** Hazard Analysis and Critical Control Point (HACCP) is a systematic preventive approach to food safety and pharmaceutical safety that addresses physical, chemical, and biological hazards as a means of prevention rather than finished product inspection.
- **Harvest Timing:** When to pick is one of the most important decision grower has to make each year.
- **Harvesting:** The date on which the grapes are picked or gathered varies according to the local customs, climate, region, location but as far as possible a spell of fine dry weather is chosen for harvesting.
- **Healthy Breakfast:** Breakfast should provide about 20-25% of daily nutritional requirements, and it's not just about having any breakfast – it's about having a healthy breakfast
- **Heat Capacity:** Heat energy required to change the temperature of a specific quantity of material
- **Heat Pump:** A refrigerant system used for heating and cooling purposes.
- **Heat Transmission Coefficient:** Quantity of heat (usually Btu in the United States) transmitted from one substance to another per unit of time (usually 1 hr) through one unit of surface (usually 1 ft2) of building material per unit of temperature difference (usually 10F).
- **Heat, Latent:** Heat associated with the change of state (phase) of a substance, for example, from a solid to a liquid (ice to water) or from a liquid to a gas (water to steam vapour).
- **Heat, Sensible:** Heat associated with a change in temperature of a substance.
- **Heat, Specific:** Ratio of the thermal capacity of a substance to the thermal capacity of water.
- **Heat, Total:** Sum of the sensible and latent heat in a substance above an arbitrary datum, usually 320F or 00C.
- **Hedging:** is a buying procedure. In this items are bought in advance at lower rate in speculation of rise in price in future.
- **Herbal Tea:** These contain no tea leaf but are made up of flowers, berries, peels, seeds and roots of plant like Camellia, Rosemary, Mint, Lemon Grass, Ginseng, Milfoil, Rose Chip Tea etc.

- **Hollowware:** The term hollowware is also a collective term for all those utensils whether apart from cutlery or crockery which used to keep or hold dishes/items, for example, water jug, entree dish, portion bowl, butter dish, etc.
- **Horizontal Communication:** Communication between employees at the same level in their own departments or other departments, to solve problems and to share experiences is called Horizontal Communication.
- **House Brand:** A brand of liquor a restaurant uses when guests orders cocktails without specifying the use of any particular brand.
- **House Wines:** Any wine which is not too expensive or too cheap and can be used by any restaurant. No particular brand is branded as house wine.
- **Humidity, Absolute:** Weight of water vapour per unit volume of a vapour-air mixture.
- **Humidity, Percent:** Ratio of humidity in a volume of air to the maximum amount of water vapour that the air can hold at a given temperature, expressed as a percentage.
- **Humidity, Relative (RH):** Ratio of the vapour pressure in a mixture of air and water vapour to the vapour pressure of the air when saturated at the same temperature.
- **Humidity, Specific (Humidity Ratio):** Ratio of the weight of water vapour, grains, or pounds, per pound of dry air, at a specific temperature.
- **Humidity:** Water vapour mixed with dry air.
- **Hygrometer:** A mechanical device used to measure the moisture content of air.
- **Hygroscopic:** Denoting any material that readily absorbs moisture and retains it.
- **Hygrostat:** A mechanical device that is sensitive to changes in humidity and used to actuate other mechanical devices when predetermined limits of humidity are reached.
- **Ice Beer:** The filtration process in beer involves chilling the beer to very low temperature so that ice crystals from in it, crystals are then removed; result is very smooth and strong beer.
- **IGP (Indication Geographique Protegée):** the European equivalent of the French VDP.
- **Incentive Travel / Incentive:** A form of group travel, paid by companies to reward their top performers or customers by sending them on unforgettable trips of a few days' duration. Incentive events are always

'live'/in-person events.

- **India pale ale (IPA):** Heavily hopped strong pale ale, originally brewed in UK for shipping to British colonies. The modern style is light coloured, hoppy ale.
- **Indian Breakfast:** India is a country of vast diversity in culture and tradition. Food being part of culture, provides a large variety of dishes in breakfast. It includes dishes like Idli-Sambhar, Vada-Sambhar, Poori-Bhaji, Chole-Bhatoore, Nahari-Kulcha, Stuffed/Plain Paratha with Curd, Poha, Khaman Dhokla with variety pickles and Chutneys.
- **Industrial Catering:** Preparation and service of food for employees working in factories at subsidized rates.
- **Informal buying-** In this method, the buyer invites quotations from the suppliers for items according to their specification. The supplies are then selected and then bought.
- **Informal Communication Network:** In this type of network, information does not flow in a particular direction, as we have seen with formal networks. The information is also not passed on through official channels such as memos, notices or bulletin boards. The information need not be circulated within the organization, but could be passed on outside the work environment, wherever co-workers or colleagues meet socially. Thus, informal networks are based more on friendship, shared personal or career interests.
- **In-house Breakfast:** In-house breakfast is generally offered by hotel at a fixed price, dishes are laid on buffet and guests are allowed to choose their favourite breakfast dishes from the buffet.
- **Inn:** A house providing food, beverage and accommodation.
- **Institutional catering:** These caterers at universities, factories and office blocks provide a wide variety of food and drink to a large number of people on an ongoing basis-usually at the institution itself. The institution usually contracts with a catering company to have this service provided.
- **Internal Control:** An accounting method, procedure, or system designed to promote efficiency, ensure the implementation of company policies, safeguard assets, and discover and avoid errors or fraud.
- **Inventory:** It refers to stock of goods.
- **Invoice:** An invoice is essentially a detailed bill left by vendors and outside suppliers for goods or services rendered to a company.

- **Irish coffee:** Black coffee, to which Irish Whisky is added, topped with whipped cream.
- **Isinglass:** Bladder of sturgeon fish used for cleaning of wine.
- **Job Analysis:** It includes identifying the nature of the Job, prerequisite skills, educational requirements and qualification required for the job.
- **Job description:** Job descriptionsare written statements that describe the duties, responsibilities, most important contributions and outcomes needed from a position.
- **Job Satisfaction:** They include the qualities and the qualification required for a particular job and may also include the years of experience.
- **Job specification:** It contains the information in relation to the qualities sought in a job candidate. Before hiring a catering department employee, a manager generally looks for various qualities like – technical skills, interpersonal skills & conceptual skills.
- **Joven Abogado:** The word literally means 'young and adulterated'. It is not 100% agave and it is not aged. It is an example of mixto.
- **Juice:** A liquid extracted from any raw food, usually fruits.
- **K.O.T.:** Kitchen order Ticket
- **Keg Cider:** It is pasteurized and filtered cider which is usually carbonated and sweetened and brilliant in appearance.
- **Labeling:** Labelling is done according to wine.
- **Labour Cost:** The amount paid to employees.
- **Lagers (Bottom Fermented Beers):** The name originates from German words "Lagern" means to store. Fermentation takes place at the bottom of the vessel and the beer is stored at low temperatures for up to six months and sometime longer. Different types of ales are following:
- **Light Bodied Wine:** The term light refers to alcoholic content, texture and weight of wine, light also refers to sensation in mouth. These are not matured in casks rather left in stainless steel or glass vats before bottling. The alcoholic content should be less than 12% for example Mâcon Blanc, Pouilly Fuissé etc.
- **Light fixture:** The base and writing that connects to an electric power source, and a reflective surface to direct the light of a bulb.
- **Light:** The wines should be stored in darkness as the light will affect the colour and darken the White Wine
- **Linen:** It consists of table cloths, napkins, tray cloths, slip cloths, buffet cloths, waiter's cloths and tea cloths used in a food and beverage service

establishment.

- **Live Event:** 'Live' events or in-person events are events whose attendees are physically present at a certain (physical) location as opposed to online or virtual events.
- **Low Alcoholic Beers (LABs):** Beer must contain less than 1.2% alcohol by volume.
- **Main Course:** It is the main dish of the menu.
- **Master Budget:** It represents the forecasted targets set for the entire organization and combines all income and expenditure estimated for the organization.
- **Maturing of Wines:** It is said that wine age in bottles and mature in the casks. Maturing takes place naturally by keeping the wine to rest in the wooden casks or barrels for one to more years according to the nature of wine, to develop flavour, aroma and colour.
- **Maturing:** Natural process of allowing the wine to rest in oak barrels to gain maturity and character.
- **Maturing:** Natural process of allowing the wine to rest in oak barrels to gain maturity and character.
- **Mechanical Harvesting:** The advantages of mechanization are reduced labour costs and a quick harvest of the entire crop at optimum ripeness, but the vineyard has to be adapted to the machine chosen and the reception and fermentation facilities must be enlarge to cope with the larger amounts and quicker throughput which is costly.
- **Medium Bodied Wine:** These are wines which are round, fairly fat with good body, texture, flavour for example Rioja (Spanish), Hermitage (French) etc.
- **Mélange:** Blend.
- **Menu Engineering:** It is a term used after considering the marketing of the present and future menu in designing and pricing. The Boston Consulting Group or BCG model is a matrix format to ascertain and analyses the business in the present scenario menu, considering the interest of the organization. It helps chef and F& B managers to plan profitable menu.
- **Menu Merchandising:** It is the process by which the menu is marketed and may include various forms of presentation, language, theme and type of operation.
- **Menu Planning:** It is a managerial activity which is marketed between the food production and service personnel having knowledge of various

cuisines, cost of preparing dishes, time for preparing dishes and the clientele.

- **Menu:** Menu is a selling tool of an establishment which may offer both food and beverages for sale. The menu has all the dishes which are available with the price quoted beside it.
- **Méthode Traditionnelle:** Traditional method of sparkling winemaking.
- **Millésime:** Vintage.
- **Mineral Water:** Usually water from natural springs impregnated with various minerals and gases.
- **Mini bar:** A small refrigerator placed in hotel rooms from which guest may obtain water bottles, beer, cold drinks and snack which is chargeable.
- **Mirror Platter:** It is the platter with a mirror finish a base and is normally used for enhanced presentations of salads and cold meats.
- **Mis en bouteille au château/domaine:** Bottled at the chateau/estate.
- **Mise en place:** It is also called as "Putting everything in its place or making ready everything" before starting service in restaurant & other food & beverage outlets.
- **Mis-en-scene:** preparation of the environment in a restaurant.
- **Mocktails:** A delicate mixture of non-alcoholic beverages possessing all qualities of a cocktail except alcohol.
- **Monkey bowl:** A small multipurpose bowl used for serving accompaniments
- **Mousseux :** Generic term for sparkling.
- **Multiplier effect:** It can also be called as "Multiple effect". In economics, the multiplier effect or spending multiplier is the idea that an initial amount of spending leads to increased consumption spending and so results in an increase in national income greater than the initial amount of spending.
- **Must :** Unfermented grape juice.
- **Napery:** Tablecloths and napkins.
- **Négociant :** A merchant who buys grapes, juice or wine from growers and sells the wines under his own label.
- **Neutral Vodka:** It is distilled from grain or potato and highly rectified. It is filtered through activated charcoal or quartz sand.
- **Noble Rot:** A mould which helps to remove moisture from grapes.
- **Noble Rot:** Noble rot also known as "Pouritture Noble" in French, "Edelfaule" in German, "Muffa" in Italian and sometimes simply

"Botrytis Cineria" (boh-TRY-tiss sin-eh-RAY-ah). The Botrytis is derived from two words of Latin origin i.e. Botrytis – meaning bunch of grapes and Cineria – meaning ashes.

- **Non Alcoholic Beers (NABs):** Beer must contain less than 0.5% alcohol by volume.
- **Non-Verbal Communication:** Non-verbal communication can be defined as communication done without speaking or writing. It involves various types of body gestures and postures.
- **Off-premises catering:** The caterer has a production facility but holds events somewhere else. The caterer transports all required food, beverages, personnel and equipment for event to a location usually choose by the client.
- **Oolong:** Chinese tea fermented for a short period of time.
- **Opportunity Cost:** It is the value of the best alternative predetermined in a situation in which a choice has to be made between several mutually exclusive alternatives with limited resources.
- **Organic Wines:** Organic wines are a wine in which no chemical are added in the soil and good example of organic wines are made by 'Listel' in carmargne region of France.
- **Organisation Internationale de MétrologieLégale (OIML):** Most countries follow OIML system. It measures the strength as percentage of volume at 20°C. OIML is same as GL which is most logical of the system.
- **Organization:** The command, control and feedback relationships among a group of people and information systems. Examples: a private company, a government agency.
- **Organizing:** Organizing includes allocating resources, allocating duties, and incorporating systems and procedures to meet the requirements or the objectives set in the planning process.
- **Pantry:** Storeroom, especially for crockery, cutlery etc.
- **Pasteurization:** This is a process of sterilizing the wine, so that the microorganism it contains is destroyed. The wine in bottles is immersed upright in double boiler with water, heated to temperatures between 180 - 190° F, the immersion is for 1-2 minutes only.
- **Payroll Analysis:** It is the process by which the salary of the staff is calculated either on a daily or monthly basis and is represented accordingly.
- **Performance Analysis:** It is the process by which employee performance is monitored after they are trained and briefed about a

particular job.

- **Perpetual Inventory:** - A perpetual inventory is a system in which the entire inventory is conducted and recorded and any additions or deletions are made to the total inventory as required and then recorded.
- **Perry:** Perry is an alcoholic beverage made from fermented juice of pears, similar to the way cider is made. In the production of Perry, it is allowed to mix cider apple juice to a maximum of 25%. Perry is carbonated either by tank method or direct impregnation method.
- **Petite Champagne** –Made entirely from brandies produced from grapes grown in the Petite Champagne region.
- **Physical Inventory:** - In a physical inventory system, an individual counts each product which is present in the store. After the inventory is taken, the value of the products held in the inventory is also ascertained.
- **Pilsner:** Clear, pale lagers (originally from Pilsen, Czech Republic hence the name). Morden styles are characterized by a zesty hop taste and bubbly body.
- **Place setting:** One person's set of flatware, plates and glassware to be arranged on a dining table.
- **Placemat:** It is a type of mat made up of paper of plastic and is used on tables with a top made of glass, wood, mica or other such finishes which are not covered with a baize cloth.
- **Planning:** Planning is a process by which various goals and objectives are prepared and framing the steps through which the goals and objectives can be attained.
- **Porter:** Since this ale was very popular amongst the porters of Dublin and London's Covent garden porters- thus the name. Porter is a dark style of beer developed in London from well hopped beer made from brown malt which contributes bitter taste and darker colour. It has a milder hop flavour, although higher in alcoholic content, it can be as much as 6-7% alcohol by volume.
- **Pour Cost:** Pour cost is calculated by simply adding up the cost of the product used and dividing it by the cost of the product sold.
- **Premier cru:** First growth. Denotes land of superior quality, but falls short of a grand cru status.
- **Premium:** Also known as top-shelf, these items are usually the most expensive and carry a more refined reputation. These bottles are often on display on your back bar or in display cases to pique customer's interest.

- **Preserves:** Jam, Jelly and Marmalade. Sometimes honey also.
- **Primary Catering:** Establishments which are primarily concerned with the service of food and beverages.
- **Propriétaire:** Estate or vineyard owner.
- **Pruning:** It is important for controlling quantity and quality. If quantity is reduced the quality increases.
- **Purchase order-** Is a formal written document which states all the specifications required for purchase of items. This order is sent to the supplier for supplying items.
- **Purchasing:** It is a procurement function concerned with search, selection, purchase, receipt, storage and final use of commodity in accordance with the catering policy of the establishment.
- **Puzzle:** A menu engineering classification of items that are particularly profitable but not very popular with the guest.
- **Racking:** Draining the clear wine off its LEES or sediments into another vat or cask is known as Racking. In modern vinification, racking is usually conducted several times throughout the maturation period in vat or cask to make a „Clear Wine", the wine gradually throws off less and less of a deposit.
- **Raisin:** Dried Grape.
- **Receiving:** Process of examining shipments to determine if they should be accepted or refused.
- **Récoltant:** Grape grower. May also refer to the person harvesting the grapes.
- **Récolte:** Harvest (may also refers to vintage).
- **Rectified Sprit:** A pure sprit e.g. Vodka, gin.
- **Red Wine:** Red wine is always made from red grapes. The skins are retained in the must during all or part of fermentation to extract the pigment from grapes giving the wine red colour.
- **Reduced Alcohol Beer:** Reduced alcohol beer is beer with little or no alcohol content. Most low alcohol beers are lagers but there are some low alcohol ales. Low alcohol beer is also known as light beer, non alcoholic beer or near-beer etc. In the U.S.A, beverages containing less than 0.5% alcohol by volume are legally called non-alcoholic beer may be legally sold to minors in many American states. In United Kingdom there are two different categories apply:
- **Refrigeration or Cold Stabilization:** The young wine is pumped into a refrigeration unit to stabilize the wine.

- **Registration Fee:** Cost of attending a conference. Fees can vary according to the time of registration, level of participation and also membership type.
- **Remwage:** Process of cleaning the wine by freezing wine bottles in wooden racks at an angle.
- **Reposado (Rested/Aged)** : It is aged in oak casks for a period of two months to one year. The same cask used for maturing Bourbon whiskey may be used for aging tequila. This process mellows the tequila and adds colour to the some extent.
- **Risk Purchase:** If supplier fails, the item is purchased from other agencies & the difference in cost is recovered from the first supplier.
- **Rosé Wine:** Rose wine is made from red grapes, never a mixture of red and white grapes, as is commonly thought. The skins are kept in must for only a short time (12-36 Hours) to impart the light pink colour.
- **Rouge:** Red.
- **Sake:** Sake is national drink of Japan. Sake is an alcoholic beverage made by fermenting rice that has been polished to remove the bran. It is brewed and fermented drink made from rice in Japan.
- **Salad Bar:** It is self – service concept in which each guest is given the opportunity to prepare his or her own salad from an attractive array of fresh vegetables and fruit that have been cleaned and sliced.
- **Salver:** Tray, usually, round and made of silver, on which drinks etc are presented.
- **Scheduling:** It is the time frame in which employees report to work, and perform and complete their work.
- **Secondary Caterings:** The provision of food and beverage is a part of another business.
- **Seminar:** most of the time organized by a private company with the intention of training and exchanging on a specific topic, the seminar gathers, without imposed regularity, professionals that may be members of this company.
- **Service area:** Service areas are platform or place where foods are kept after final cooking, so that steward come & receive the prepared food & serve to the guest.
- **Service of Cigars:** Cigar should be offered in their own boxes to allow the guest to choose his own. The type of cigar will be printed on box. The guest having chosen the cigar he/she wishes, the server should offer to remove the band. A cigar cutter should be used to cut the cigar. The

server should then offer to light the cigar of guests. (Cigar should be offered at the end of meal with coffee)

- **Serviette:** It is a type of cloth which is used by the stewards during service.
- **SGN (Sélection de Grains Nobles):** Selection of noble berries. Refers to wines made from grapes affected by noble rot, or botrytized. SGN wines are sweet dessert wines with rich, concentrated flavours. Some of the finest botrytized wines are literally picked berry by berry in successive *"tries"* (French for selections).
- **Side Board:** furniture central to an operation at a station.
- **Sikes Scale:** It is used in Britain and the commonwealth countries. Bartholomew sykes introduced a hydrometer which calculated that 57.1% of alcohol is equivalent to 100° proof. So 100% alcohol is equal to 175° proof.
- **Silverware:** A term used for cutlery made up of silver or plated silver.
- **Smoking Cigars:** There is an art involved in smoking a cigar, it should never be inhaled. The end with joins the mouth is "V" shaped or straight cut with care and never bitten off. The paper band must be removed before smoking a cigar. The cigar is then lit evenly all sides with a match and never with a lighter, which may taint it with aroma of spirit. The butt end is bitter due to the accumulation of oil and tannin, therefore cigar is never smoked to the end.
- **Sommeliers:** This is the person to handle the ordering and serving of wine. They must be thoroughly knowledgeable about their own wine lists and competent in helping guest to select wine appropriate to the food they order.
- **Soup tureen:** Deep Covered dish from which soup is served at the table using a ladle.
- **Sparkling Wine:** These are sparkling in appearance due to presence of CO2 gas and thus give off bubbles of gas. The best known is "champagne", it is produced by a complicated process. Sparkling wine is one where natural gas from fermentation is retained in the bottle or one where the wine has been artificially impregnated with gas.
- **Specialty restaurant:** A fine dining out let in which service is both formal and stylish.
- **Spiced Rum:** it is dark in colour, flavoured, and coloured with spices and caramel. Inexpensive white rum may be coloured with liberal caramel.

- **Squash:** Edible fruit of the gourd family, divided into two categories – (1) summer (2) winter.
- **Stakeholder:** An individual or group with an interest in the success of an organization in delivering intended results and maintaining the viability of the organization's products and services. Stakeholders influence programs, products, and services
- **Standard Buffet:** Platters or chafing dishes of food are placed on centralized tables and guest serves themselves.
- **Standard Cost:** This is the cost of a product worked out for a standard portion.
- **Standard Recipe:** A standard of recipe is prepared by every establishment so that each chef/bartenders prepares the dish/drink with the same ingredients..
- **Standard yield-** Standard Yield of a particular food item may be defined as usable part of that particular food product after initial preparation, or the edible part of the product after preparation and cooking.
- **Stateroom:** A private cabin on a passenger ship.
- **Station:** A set of four or five table in a restaurant.
- **Still wine:** Wine which lacks carbonation.
- **Stopover/transfer:** when a group of passengers stay for more than 24 hours at the same place, we use the word stopover. If the passenger does not leave the airport or stays less than 24 hours in the country, we use the word transfer.
- **Stout:** Stout has high hop content and a strong malt taste. The malt used for stout is also first roasted, which gives this beer its very dark colour. Has a smooth malty flavour and creamy consistency. One of the best known stouts is Guinness of Ireland.
- **Suggestive Selling:** A sales technique used by servers to increase guest satisfaction and sales by encouraging guests to order extras like appetizers, cocktails, mocktails, desserts etc.
- **Sulphuring:** It is frequently necessary to add $SO_2\uparrow$ fairly early in the fermentation process to prevent the air from oxidizing the must and converting the alcohol into vinegar.
- **Supérieur:** Wine with higher (superior) alcohol content as a result of being made fromriper grapes.
- **Sweet Wine:** Sweet wine produced by grapes having high sugar content, as in these wines even after fermentation a lot of sugar is still left, which is not consumed by yeast, the sugar left renders a very sweet wine.

- **Table d hote** - It is a restricted menu, offering small number of course with limited choice of food in each course, fix selling price and dishes being ready at a set time.
- **Table d'hote Menu:** Table d'hote menu is a restricted menu, offering a small number of courses (three of four) a limited choice within each course, fixed selling price and all the dishes being ready at a set time.
- **Tableware:** A term used for all pieces of flatware, cutlery and hollowware.
- **Tender-** This type of formal buying method. In this sealed structural documents invited by organization from respective sellers for a fixed type of item and according to fixed specification.
- **Trappist:** Beer brewed in Trappist monasteries, usually under the supervision of monks. It is a kind of strong beer with 6-12% alcohol by volume; six Belgian breweries produce this beer, which is complex and unpasteurized.
- **Traveller's Cheques:** These are issued by reputed banks to avoid the risk of carrying cash.
- **Triplicate Method:** in this method the order is taken in three copies. The top copy goes to the supply point, second copy is sent to the cashier for billing; third copy is retained by the server as a means of reference during service.
- **Ullage:** It is the space between the cork and the top of the wine. It is also referred as weeping wine.
- **Under bar:** This is the area inside the bar counter, under the front bar, which holds the essential equipments and liquor supplies required for making drinks.
- **Upward Communication:** It is non directive in nature. Effective upward communication is possible only when organizations empower their employees and allow them to participate freely in decision making. Through this type of communication employees can communicate information to their superiors freely and can voice their opinion.
- **Variable Cost:** The cost which tends to vary indirect proportion to change in the volume of output or turnover.
- **Varietal Wines:** These are the wines of North America, which are labelled after the main grapes variety in the bottle. Single grape variety is used for making wine, best known examples are:
- **Venue Manager:** The person in charge of a location or event space.
- **Venue:** A place to hold your event.

- **Verbal Communication:** Communication done through spoken words is called verbal communication
- **Vertical communication:** Vertical communication occurs between various hierarchies. It may be upward or downward. For example manager to employee, general manager to managers, foreman to machine operator, head of the department to cashiers, etc.
- **Vibration:** The wines should be permitted to sleep peacefully without agitation. The bottles should be completely still. There should be no vibrations of the floor.
- **Vine Training:** The manner in which a vine is trained will guide the size, shape and height of the plant towards reaping maximum benefits from the local conditions of aspects and climate. Vines can be trained high to avoid ground frost or low to hug any heat that may be reflected by stony soils at night.
- **Vinification:** The process which converts grapes into wine.
- **Vintage Wines:** The French word "vintage" means harvest, although any wine is a vintage wine as any year can be vintage year. However some year's climate is so good that the government in France declares it as vintage year for particular region.
- **Vintage:** Year when the grapes density is constant, hence quality of wine is superior to wine from other year.
- **Viticulture Sprays:** The use of sprays was once confined to protecting the vine against pests and diseases and for controlling weeds but now they have addition uses. Some sprays deliberately induce two disorder called Millerandage and Coulure to reduce the yield and increase quality.
- **Waffles and pancakes:** Waffles and pancakes, also called *griddle cakes* and *hot cakes*, are made from pourable batters. Pancakes are made on a griddle, while waffles are made on a special tool called a *waffle iron*.
- **Waiter's friend:** Tool that is a combination of bottle opener and corkscrew.
- **Weighing:** The grapes are weighed to determine the quantity required for fermentation.
- **Welcome Signage:** A sign that introduces or welcomes visitors to the venue / event.
- **Well:** Spirits used when patrons don't name a spirit brand in a drink order. (Example: Gin and tonic). Your well bottles are often the best deal for both the bar and the customer.

- **White and Light Rum:** It has very little flavour and is colourless. Its colourless and flavourless feature has made this variety perfect ingredient for cocktails. Most of the white rums come from Puerto Rico.
- **White Wine:** White wine is made from white grapes, in rare cases also made from red grapes.
- **Wine:** An alcoholic beverage made from partial or complete fermentation of grape juice.
- **Work flow.** A workflow consists of a sequence of connected steps. It is a depiction of a sequence of operations, declared as work of a person, a group of persons, an organization of staff, or one or more simple or complex mechanisms.
- **Workshop:** workshops generally have more hands-on and group activities. The sessions are quite interactive and require individuals to participate.
- **Wrapper:** Wrapper or outer covering of cigar consists of a ribbon leaf rolled spirally around the cigar bunch. Wrapper leaf must be strong, elastic and silky in texture and of even colour and it must possess good flavour and burning properties. It is most expensive leaf used in cigars.
- **Yield management.** Yield management is the practice of maximizing profits from the sale of perishable items like food, hotel rooms / airline seats, by controlling price and inventory and differentiating product & service.
- **Zero-based Budgeting:** It involves budgeting from the beginning without any reference to historical data.

# CHAPTER TWO

# Career in Front Offices

## *An Overview of Room Division*

### *Room Division:*

The room division comprises departments and personnel essential to providing the services guest expect during a hotel stay. In most hotels, the rooms division generates more revenue than all other divisions combined. The front office is one department within the rooms division. Others are housekeeping, uniformed services, and the concierge. In some properties, the reservations and switchboard or telephone functions are separate departments within the rooms division. Figure at previous page shows a sample organization chart for the rooms division of a large hotel.

### *The Front Office*

This is the most visible department in a hotel. Front office personnel have more contact with guest than do staff in most other departments. The front desk is usually the focal point of activity for the front desk to register; to receive room assignments, to inquire about available services, facilities, and the control center for guest requests concerning housekeeping or engineering issues. Foreign guest use the front desk to exchange currency, find a translator, or request other special assistance. In addition, it may also be base of operations during an emergency, such as a fire or a guest injury. The functions of the front office are to:

1. Sell guestrooms, register guests, and assign guestrooms.

2. Process future room reservations, when there is no reservation department or when the reservation department is closed.

3. Coordinate guest services.

4. Provide information about the hotel, the surrounding community, and any attractions or events of interest to guest.

5. Maintain accurate room status information. Maintain guest and monitor credit limits.

6. Produce guest account statements and complete proper financial settlement.

## *Uniformed Service*

Employees who work in the uniformed service department of the hotel generally provide the most personalized guest service. Given the high degree of attention awarded guest by this department, some properties refer to uniformed service simply as guest service. Among the primary positions within the uniformed service department are:

1. Bell attendant – persons who provide baggage service between the lobby area and the guestroom.

2. Door attendants – persons who provide curb-side baggage service and traffic control at the hotel entrance.

3. Valet parking attendants-persons who provide parking service for guest's vehicles.

4. Transportation personnel – persons who provide transportation service for guests.

5. Concierges – person who assist guest by making restaurant reservations, arranging for transportation, and getting for tickets for theater, sporting, or other special events, and so on.

**Bell Attendants**: many guests arrive at a hotel with heavy baggage or several pieces of luggage. Guest receives help handling this luggage from probably the best-known employee among the uniformed service staff: the bell attendant. Bell attendant should be clearly selected. Since most hotels have carts for transporting baggage, the physical ability to actually carry the baggage is not a critical job qualification. More important, bell attendants should have strong oral communication skills and display genuine interest in ach guest. Depending on the size and complexity of the hotel, bell attendants may be counted on to:

1. Transport guest luggage to and from guestrooms.

2. Familiarize guest with the hotel's facilities and services, safety features, as well as the guestroom and any in-room amenities.

3. Provide a secure area for guest requiring temporary luggage storage.

4. Provide information on hotel services and facilities, as well as group functions.

5. Deliver mail, packages, messages, and special amenities to guestrooms.

6. Pick up and deliver guest laundry and dry cleaning.

7. Perform light housekeeping services in lobby and entry areas.

8. Help guest load and unload their luggage in the absence of a door attendant.

9. Notify other departments of guest needs, such as housekeeping for a crib or extra towels.

While many of these tasks appear simple, they all require a degree of professionalism. For example to assist a guest with his or her luggage, the belt attendant must know how to properly load a luggage cart. Fragile items must not be placed below heavy items. The cart must also be properly balanced so that it does not tip over or become difficult to steer. It is through informal conversation that bell attendants become key players in the hotel's guest's names. This makes guests feel more welcome and allows the bell attendant to provide more personal service.

**Door Attendants**

Door attendants play a role similar to bell attendants; they are dedicated to welcoming the guest to the hotel. These employees are generally found in hotels offering world-class or luxury service of the duties door attendants perform include:

1. Opening hotel doors and assisting guest upon arrival.

2. Helping guest load and unload luggage from vehicles.

3. Escorting guests to the hotel registration area.

4. Controlling vehicle traffic flow and safety at the hotel entrance.

5. Hailing taxis, upon request.

6. Performing light housekeeping services in the lobby and entry areas.

Experienced door attendants are capable of handling all these tasks with aplomb. A skilled and experienced door attendant learns the names of the frequent guest. When these guest returns to the hotel, the door attendant is able to greet them by name and can introduce them to other front office staff. Such personal service enhances the reputation of the hotel and provides the guest with as unique experience.

**Valet parking attendants**

Valet parking is generally available at hotels offering world-class or luxury service. Specially trained employees park guest and visitor automobiles. Thpersonal attention and security of valet parking service is considered both a luxury and a convenience. Guest does not have to worry about finding a parking space, walking to the hotel in inclement weather, or finding their vehicles in the parking lot. Hotels generally charge a higher fee for valet parking, guest are also likely to tip the valet parking attendant.

The uniformed service department is responsible for all vehicles under its care and reports information to the front desk each night so that parking charges can be posted to guest accounts. In addition, when the vehicle entrance to the hotel is busy, valet parking attendants should help keep the area running smoothly by providing traffic control assistance.

### Concierges

Even though this guest service position has existed for quite some time, the concierge is perhaps the concierge was the castle doorkeeper. A concierge's job was to ensure that all the castle occupants were secure in their rooms at night. Traveling royalty was often accompanied by a concierge who provided security and traveled ahead of the royal party to finalize food and lodging arrangements. As hotels became more common in Europe, the concierge eventually became apart of the staff that provided personalized guest services. It is not uncommon to find a concierge at a world-class or luxury hotel.

Concierges may provide custom services to hotel guest. Duties include making reservations for dining securing tickets for theater and sporting events; arranging for transportation, and providing information on cultural events and local attractions. Concierges are known for their resourcefulness. Getting tickets to sold out concerts or making last-minute dinner reservations at a crowded restaurant are part of a concierge's responsibility and reputation. Most successful concierges have developed an extensive network of local, regional, and national contacts the concierge has established at restaurants, box office, car rentals offices,, airlines , printers, and other businesses. Some hotels actually encourage concierges to visit appropriate businesses and organizations to establish and strengthen such relationships. Finally, a highly successful concierge should speak several languages.

### Housekeeping

Housekeeping is perhaps the most important support department for the front office. Like the front office, housekeeping usually is part of the rooms division of the hotel. In some hotels, however, the housekeeping function is considered an independent hotel division. Effective communication among housekeeping and front office personnel can contribute to guest satisfaction while helping the front office to effectively monitor guestroom status. Housekeeping employees inspect rooms before they are available for sale, clean occupied and vacated rooms, and communicate the status of guestroom until the room has been cleaned, inspected and released by the housekeeping department.

The housekeeping department often employs larger staff than other departments i.e. the rooms division. Normally, an executive housekeeper is in charge of the department, aided by an assistant housekeeper. In larger hotels there can be several assistant housekeepers, each responsible for specific floors, sections, or, in room attendants, lobby and general cleaners, and laundry personnel. Room attendant are assigned to specific sections nof the hotel. Depending on the hotel's service level, average guestroom size, and cleaning tasks, room attendants may clean from 8 to 18 rooms per shift. If the hotel has its own laundry, housekeeping department staff may be charged with cleaning and pressing the property's linens, towels, uniforms, and guest clothing. Housekeeping personnel (usually executive housekeepers) are responsible for maintaining two types of inventories: recycled and non-recycled. Recycled inventories are those items that have a relatively limited useful life but are used repeatedly in housekeeping operations. Theses inventories include such items as linens, uniforms, and guest amenities like irons and hair dryers. Non-recycled inventories are those items that are consumed or worn out during the course of routine housekeeping operations. Non-recycled inventories include cleaning supplies, small equipment items, and guest supplies and personnel grooming items. Guest amenities and m\linens are among the items and conveniences most often requested by guests.

To ensure the speedy, efficient rooming of guest in vacant and inspected room, the housekeeping and front office departments must promptly inform each other of any change in a room' status or availability. Team work between housekeeping and the front office is essential to effective hotel operations. To more familiar housekeeping and front office personnel are with each other's departmental procedures, the smoother the relationships.

**<u>Standard layout of front office department and its sections:</u>**

Division of labor is the guiding principle for dividing the entire unit into small section on the basis of tasks performed by the employees of the department. The front office department can be divided in to following sections for effective and efficient discharge of the duties of its employees:

- Reservation
- Reception
- Information
- Cash & bills
- Travel desk
- Communication
- Uniformed services

  - Bell Desk
  - Concierges

**Lobby**

According to Oxford dictionary, _lobby is an area just inside a large building, where people can meet and wait'. The hotel lobby is an area furnished with seating arrangements and is used as common place for meeting and waiting by the hotel guests. Lobby is located immediately upon entry into the hotel building. The front office is located within the premises of the lobby. The lobby is an important place in the hotel as it is the first and last point of guest contact with hotel. Hence, a considerable amount of fund is invested by the owner to make the lobby aesthetically appealing to the guest. A well appointed lobby creates the impression about the overall standard of the hotel in the eyes of the guest. The lobby is managed by the lobby manager.

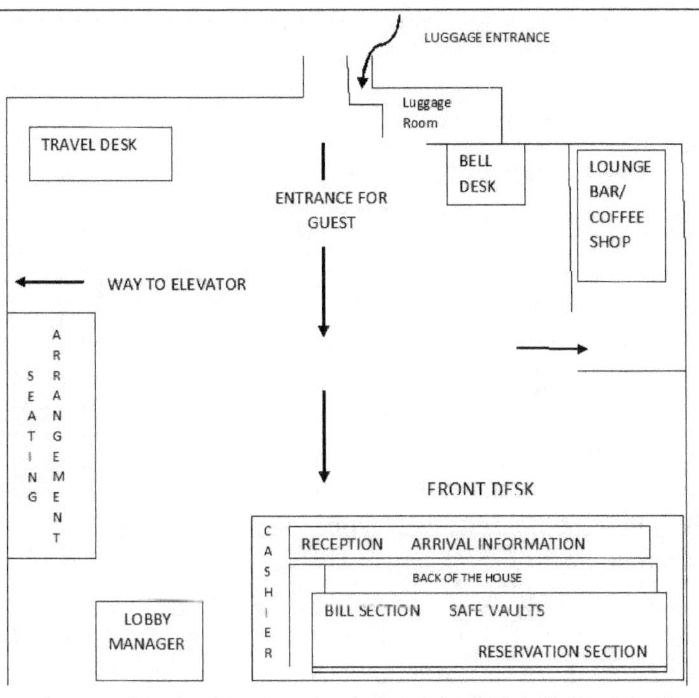


## LAYOUT OF FRONT OFFICE DEPARTMENT

**<u>Organization structure of hotel with special reference to front office department:</u>**

The front office staff organization is deliberately designed to achieve objectives of the organization. It refers to the structure of well defined jobs, each bearing a definite authority, responsibility, and accountability. The organization structure is built upon the following pillars:

- Division of labour
- Span of control

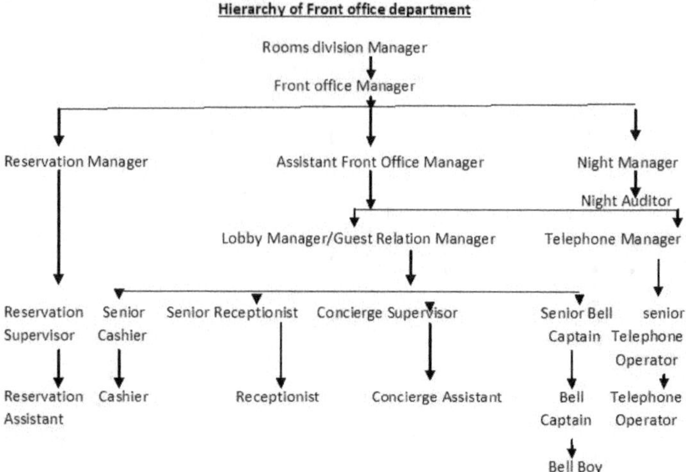


## Duties and responsibilities of front office employees:

Guests remain in direct contact with the front office staff throughout their stay at the hotel. As the front office personnel are the first and last point of contact with the guest, they reflect the image of the hotel and hence should carry themselves and behave in a way which fits the vision of the organization.

Following are the qualities of front office personnel which is needed to be efficient on their duties:-

- Pleasing Personality
- Personal Hygiene
- Physical Fitness
- Honesty
- Salesmanship
- Diplomacy
- Good Memory
- Good Communication Skills
- Calmness
- Courteous
- Loyalty
- Punctuality

### *CONCIERGE:*

A concierge is a hotel employee who provides information and personalised services to the guest like dinner reservation, tour and travel arrangements and obtaining tickets for special events in the city. A concierge is often expected to achieve the impossible; dealing with any request a guest may have, relying on the various contacts with various merchants and service providers.

*The concept of Concierge came from the day of European royalty. The concierge was the castle door keeper in that time. His duty was to ensure that all castle occupants were safe in their rooms at night. When royal family travels, they often took their concierge with them for security and for making food and lodging facilities.*

As the hotel industry grew, concierge became the part of hotel staff to provide personalise services to hotel's guest.

**<u>FUNCTION OF CONCIERGE:</u>**

Concierge provides following services to the guest:-

- Making reservations for dining in famous restaurants.
- Obtaining tickets for theatres, musical, sporting events etc.
- Arranging for transportation by Limousine, car, coaches, buses, etc.
- Providing information on cultural and social events like photo exhibition, art shows and local places of tourist interest.

***<u>BELL BOY:</u>***

Bell boys transport the guest luggage at the time of check in and check out. They also escort guests to their rooms and familiarize them with the room facilities and services provided by the hotel.

***<u>DUTIES & RESPONSIBILTIES OF BELL BOY:</u>***

**<u>The major duties and responsibilities of bell boy are:-</u>**

- Handles the guest luggage i.e. transport, a guest luggage from lobby to room at the time of check in, and from room to vehicle at the time of departure.
- Put luggage tag at the time of arrival of the guest
- Escort guest to their rooms and familiarize them with the facilities and electronic equipments to be used.
- When collecting luggage at the time of checkout, take a look inside the room in a hospitable manner to ensure everything is at its place.
- Keep the record of left luggage room

- Inform about the suspected scanty baggage guest at the time of check in.
- Help in locating guest in specified area within the hotel premises.
- Delivers mails, packages and messages to guest in their rooms.

### *Functions of Reservations:*

- Receiving reservation requests through various means like telephones, fax, e-mail, sales representatives or central reservation systems.
- Processing reservation request received from all means , on PMS (Property Management System).
- Depending upon the availability of the desired room type and projected sales during and around the requested stay dates, the reservation request may be confirmed, waitlisted or denied
- Updating the room availability status after each reservation transactions.
- Maintaining and updating reservation records.
- Preparing reservation reports for the management.

### *Functions of Reception:*

- Receiving and welcoming guest.
- Completing the registration formalities.
- Assigning the room
- Sending arrival notification slips to the concern departments.

### *Functions of Cash & Bills (Cashier)*

- Opening and maintaining guest folios.
- Posting room charges and guest folios.
- Recording all credit charges in guest folios.
- Maintaining a record of cash received from guest.
- Preparing bills at the time of check out.
- Receiving cash/travellers cheque/cheque/demand draft for account settlement.
- Handling credit/debit/cash cards.
- Organising foreign currency exchange for the settlement of the guest account.

### *Function of Travel Desk*

- Arranging pick up and drop services for guest at the time of their arrival and departure.
- Arranging for the guides who can communicate in guest's language.
- Organising sightseeing tours in and around the city.
- Making travel arrangements like railway and air tickets.

### *Function of Information Desk*

- Answering incoming calls. Directing calls to the guest room through EPBX system.
- Providing information services.
- Processing guest wake up calls.
- Answering enquiries about hotel facilities and events.
- Coordinating emergency communication.

# *Personality traits of front office employees:*

Most often, a front desk employee is the first person with whom a guest comes in contact. The guest starts building the image of the hotel from the physical appearance and personality of the front office personal. The gestures, grooming, and personal presentation of a front desk employee are very important in leaving a good impression in the mind of the guest. The front desk personnel should be well turned out; they should have a pleasant personality, greeting guests with a smiling face and showing interest in their concerns.

*Qualities of front office personnel:*

**Physical Fitness:** A front office employee must be physically fit to mange long hours on his feet. During peak business time or shortage of staff they may have to work at long stretches. Front office professionals must bring in physical fitness regimes into their personal lives.

**Personal Hygiene:** Front office employees should follow the highest standards of personal hygiene. The front office staff is the first point of physical contact to a guest with the hotel. A good sense of hygiene is very important for them as their appearance influences the image of the hotel. The staff need to look their best at all the times.

**Pleasant Personality:** A front desk employee is the first person whom a guest comes in contact. The gesture, grooming and personal presentation are very important for front office staff for leaving a good impression on guest.

**Diplomacy:** It is very important characteristic for front office staff. They should be very diplomatic in attending the guest's complaints for hotel or hotel services. If front office employee has to reject a room booking request, he should do that work diplomatically, without upsetting or offending the guest.

**Calmness:** The front office should be able to remain calm in high pressure situations. In some situations it happens that guest become unsatisfied or angry because of some problem in the services or products offered by the hotel to the guest at that time it is required that the front office staff deal calmly with the guest. The calmness of the front office staff in such situations will help to diffuse the tension and resolve the problem of guest.

**Loyalty:** The front office staff should be loyal to their job, as well as for the hotel and the management loyalty develops a sense of belongingness among the staff, which reflect in their behaviours with guest.

**Good Communication Skill:** The front office staff must possess good communication skill because they have to interact with guests at the time of their arrival, during their stay and also at the time of departure. They should be polite, confident and clear in their communication. They should be good in English, if they know a foreign language then that will be an advantage for them.

**Salesmanship:** They should possess salesmanship quality. They can motivate guest to increase their length of stay. They should be equipped with complete knowledge about hotel.

**Good Memory:** The front office staff must possess good memory because guests like to be recognized by the hotel staff and addressed by their names. A good memory will help the front office staff to remember and respond to the reservation requests and special preferences of guests. This gives a personalized touch and establishes a lasting relationship with the guest.

**Honesty:** They should be honest and trustworthy. Honest employees are an asset to an organization and build a good impression of hotel in guest's mind.

**Courteousness:** During interaction with guest it is important that a front office staff should be courteous and polite. They should never agree with the guest. A smooth resolution of problems teamed with the courteous behaviour of the hotel staff will develop a good will among guest.

## *Front office equipment (non-automated, semi-automated & fully automated) :*

### NON AUTOMATED

- Front Desk
- Lobby desk
- Bell desk
- Travel desk
- Page board
- GRC cabinet
- Cashier well/bucket
- Luggage Trolley
- Bell Hop Trolleys
- Luggage net

### SEMI AUTOMATED

- Date & time punching machine
- Credit card imprinter
- Telephone
- Telex machine
- Facsimile machine
- Billing and posting machine
- Photocopying machine
- Safe vault

### AUTOMATED

- POS machine (Point of Sale), computer system with advance softwares and networking

- Laser Printers
- EPABX System
- EDC machine (Electronic Data Capturing machine)
- Magnetic Strip Reader for Card Key

# Coordination of front office with other departments and sections:

The front office department play an important role in delivering quality service to the guest. Front office coordinates with various departments for smooth operations of the hotel. The below listed are the few departments with which Front office department coordinates with:-

## HOUSEKEEPING:

The front office and housekeeping departments communicate with each other for the following information:-

### Room Status:-

As rooms generate maximum revenue for hotels, the information about hte room status should be updated correctly and frequently. The front office and housekeeping departments must closely coordinated on the room status. The housekeeping department preapares an occupancy report, which is sent to the front office department where it is tallied with room status records of front desk. This helps to :-

- *Updates room status.*
- *Find Sleepers.*
- *To know the exact House Count.*
- *Charge the guest if an extra person has occupied the room.*
- *Coordinates in Guest room change requests.*

### Security Concerns:-

The housekeeping personnel should inform the front office about any unusal circumstances that may indicate a violation of security for the hotel guests. Also Front office department informs Housekeeping department about the Scanty Baggage guests to keep an eye, if something security violation of the hotel is taking place. It is the duty of Front office personnel to inform In house or civil authorities to ensure the safety and security of the guests.

**Special Arrangements:-**

Guests may requests for additional or special amenities during their stay, like extra blanket, towel etc. When such requests are received at front desk, they should be immediately conveyed to the housekeeping department. For special guests the front office may request the housekeeping department to put extra amenities in the guest room like flower arrangement, bath robe etc. The front desk also informs the housekeeping department to make special arrangements for VIPs, SPATT, groups and crews

***F&B DEPARTMENT:***

Front office department informs the F&B department about the arrival and departure of guests, which helps them to plan their work schedule and staff requirement. It also notifies the F&B department about special food arrangements and parties. The front office department usually send the following information:-

- *The arrival & Departure of the Guests.*
- *Setting of Bars in VIP's room*
- *In house and expected VIP List*
- *The scanty baggage and NO post Status Guest.*
- *Groups and Guests with Bookings of Specific meal Plan.*

Also F&B department shares information related to security concerns found during in room dining. They also inform Front office departments about banquet bookings through Function Prospectus.

***ENGINEERING & MAINTENANCE:***

The front office department communicates with engineering and maintenance department for the proper upkeep of the equipments and systems installed in the hotel. The front office informs the maintenance department of any repair work required in guest rooms. In case the maintenance activity is required in a room which is occupied by a guest, the two departments work out a schedule so that the maintenance work is carried out in the absence of the guest. But if the extensive work needs to be done, the guest may be requested to change the room.

***SECURITY:***

The front office informs about scanty baggage and doubtful guests to security department to keep an eye on their rooms. When a guest has security concerns like unlocking of double locked door, fire, robbery, theft and any other emergency, the front desk should explain the emergency procedure to the guest while calling on security personnel to resolve the problem.

### *ACCOUNTS:*

The front office department closely works with accounts department for handling Non guest accounts, back debt accounts, credit card accounts etc.

### *SALES & MARKETING:*

Though nowadays, Front office is having its own team of sales and marketing which closely deals with following:-

- *Guest History*
- *Probable Guests*
- *Offers & Packages*
- *Advertisement of Rooms & Events etc.*

For successful Optimum booking, Sales and marketing department plays an important role for the Hotel.

### *HUMAN RESOURCE:*

Front office coordinates with HR department for the requirement of new staffs, training of existing staffs, and requirement of Industrial & Vocational Trainees etc. On the guidelines regarding Job Specifications received from Front Office department, HR department floats or conducts Interviews for the recruitment of eligible staffs for Front Office Department.

## *Every FRONT OFFICE aspirant need to solve these questions to become Industry Ready:*

1. When arranging equipment at the front desk, what factors should be considered?
2. Why is the position of the front desk in a hotel lobby important?
3. Describe the evolving role of computers in the hotel industry.
4. Explain in your own words what a property management system is. How does a property management system help to provide hospitality to a guest?

5. Why should a needs analysis be performed before computers are purchased? What are the components of a needs analysis?

6. Why are computer software considerations more important than computer hardware considerations?

7. If you are employed at a hotel that uses a property management system, which of the software options listed in the text do you use? Explain the advantages of these modules.

8. If you are employed in a hotel with a property management system, discuss computer hardware descriptions with your front office manager. What does your manager find most valuable? Why?

9. Why is interfacing important in a property management system? What are some examples of interfacing?

10. What is ergonomics? How does the ergonomics of computer terminals affect the front office staff?

11. How would you go about verifying vendor claims when considering the purchase of a property management system?

12. How does a well-developed installation plan for a property management system assist hotel management?

13. Why should management be sure employees are properly trained to use a property management system?

14. If the power goes out in a 200-room lodging property for four hours, how would you preserve the data in a property management system?

15. If you are employed in a hotel, ask your front office manager if there is a maintenance agreement for the property management system. What items are covered? How well has the computer company stood behind the agreement?

16. Discuss the "purchase versus lease" consideration in terms of financial profitability.

17. What does the main menu of a PMS tell an operator? How is it organized?

18. Review the computer applications described in this chapter. Explain how they are used to provide better service to the guest and to improve financial control in the hotel.

19. How does a well-organized reservation system meet the needs of the traveller?

20. How does the lodging industry meet the needs of the traveller for assured reservations?

21. What advantages does a hotel belonging to a reservation/referral system enjoy?

22. What are some major sources of guest reservations? What information does this analysis reveal?

23. Discuss the nature of a typical corporate client's travel plans and explain how these plans are related to a well-organized reservation system. What are some reservation access methods available to the corporate client?

24. Why are tour or meeting planners important to the hotel with regard to group reservations? What are some reservation access methods available to the planner of group tours?

25. How does the pleasure traveller differ from the corporate client and group traveller?

26. What are some reservation access methods available to the pleasure traveller?

27. If you have been or are currently employed at a front desk in a hotel, what do you think of the potential for repeat business from current guests? Does your hotel have a procedure to secure reservations on check-in or checkout?

28. Why is it necessary to prepare rooms forecast? What are the components of this management tool? In addition to the front office manager, who else uses the room forecast?

29. What does "overbooking" mean? Discuss the legal and financial implications of this practice.

30. What are the components of an aggressive occupancy management procedure? How are they applied to the occupancy management formula?

31. What are the major steps involved in processing a guest reservation?

32. Briefly describe the method used to process a reservation with a computerized system.

33. Discuss the differences between a confirmed reservation and a guaranteed reservation. What financial implications does each entail?

34. Design a reservation code for a computerized reservation system. Why did you choose the control features in your code?

35. Develop a cancellation code for a computerized reservation system. Why did you choose the control features in your code?

36. What does blocking of rooms involve? Give some examples.

37. How do you think true integration of the central reservation system and a hotel's property management system will affect guest satisfaction and

the hotel's financial success?

38. How important do you think the guest's first contact with the hotel is in providing hospitality? Give some examples from your experiences as a guest in a hotel.

39. Why is obtaining guest data accurately during the registration process so important? Who uses these guest data besides the front office? Give some examples of how incorrect data can affect the guest and the hotel.

40. What are the major parts of the guest registration process? How will knowledge of this system help you as you progress in a management career in the hotel?

41. Why is the choice of credit cards important to the profit-and-loss statement of the hotel? Give some examples.

42. What are some of the hidden costs involved in using a bill-to-account system? When do you think a hotel is justified in adopting a bill-to-account system?

43. Identify some of the requests a guest will have with regard to room selection. How can a front desk clerk be attuned to the needs of a guest?

44. Why are establishing and monitoring room rates so essential to the hotel's profit and loss statement?

45. What are the rule-of-thumb method and the Hubbart's formula for establishing room rates? How effective do you feel each one is in ensuring profit for a hotel?

46. Describe a system of monitoring room rates. If you are employed at a front desk, do you see your supervisor or manager using such a system? How often? How effective do you feel this is in maintaining effective room rates?

47. Describe the various types of room rates. If you were asked by the front office manager to determine which room rates should be eliminated and whether any new types of room rates should be initiated, how would you proceed?

48. What do you think of the room rate maximization program described in the chapter? How does it affect the profit-and-loss statement? What are the important components of this program?

49. What are some opportunities for the desk clerk to sell hotel services as discussed in this chapter? If you are employed at the front desk of a hotel, do you see this being done? What effect does this have on the profit-and-loss statement?

50. What pointers would you give a new desk clerk on room key assignment?

51. Explain how to use the PMS to register a guest with a reservation. Note any inefficiency.

52. Discuss the advantages and disadvantages of registering guests with a PMS.

53. List some assets that a student may hold. List some liabilities that a student may incur. What differentiates the two terms?

54. In your own words, define the bookkeeping terms debit and credit. What power do they have in a bookkeeping context?

55. What forms are used in the various departments and the front office to provide records of a guest's charges and payments? Describe each. What are the purposes of these forms?

56. What is an electronic folio? How would you describe this to a front desk clerk who just started to use a PMS?

57. What is the guest ledger? Give an example of something included in it. Describe how you would post a check for prepayment of two nights' room rate.

58. What is the city ledger? Give an example of something included in it. Describe how you would post a check for prepayment of a social reception.

59. Give examples of the various financial transactions that may occur during a guest stay.

60. Give examples of the various financial transactions in which the nonregistered guest may be involved.

61. If you are employed in a hotel that uses a property management system that interfaces with a point-of-sale department, describe the procedure for posting a guest charge or payment.

62. Why the guest and city ledgers are considered only temporary holding areas for financial transactions? Where such records are permanently maintained?

63. Why is careful and accurate posting of charges and payments so important to the night audit? How can a front office manager ensure that posting is done correctly?

64. Why should a front office manager be concerned about compiling a guest' s late charges? Give an example of losses that can result if late charges go unpaid.

65. Why should a front desk clerk ask a guest who is checking out about the quality of products and services? Who needs this information?

66. Why is the retrieval of a room key so important to the guest? To the hotel?

67. Do you feel a guest should review the guest folio during checkout? Why?

68. If you have used an in-room guest checkout system while you were a guest in a hotel, describe the procedure you followed. Do you feel it was a convenience or a novelty?

69. Discuss the various methods of payment available to the guest. Why does the hotel not consider these payment options financially equal?

70. Discuss the various types of credit cards. Explain their advantages to the guest and to the hotel.

71. What does bill-to-account mean? What are the hidden costs involved with this method of payment?

72. Why is cash not an eagerly sought method of payment?

73. What is a debit card? How does it differ from a credit card?

74. Summarize the procedures to follow when accepting credit cards, bill-to-accounts, cash, checks, and traveller's checks as methods of payment.

75. A guest wants to pay her account of U.S. $439 in Canadian dollars. How would you proceed?

76. How do you feel about obtaining a reservation at the time of checkout? What steps would you suggest to a front office manager to secure future reservations?

77. Why will the night auditor want all paperwork in order before beginning the night audit?

78. Why must the front office communicate a guest's departure to the various point-of sale areas not interfaced with a PMS?

79. What types of guest accounts would be transferred to the back office?

80. List the various reports that can be generated by the checkout procedure and explain how they can assist management.

81. Discuss the role of the guest history in developing strategies by the marketing and sales department.

82. How important do you think hospitality is to a guest in a hotel? If you are employed in a hotel, ask your manager how he or she feels about the importance of providing hospitality to a guest.

83. How would you develop a service strategy statement? Why is this important first step in the planning process?

84. Why should frontline employees be involved in the development of a service management program?

85. How would you apply TQM to a particular situation at your place of employment? What challenges do you think will be presented in the application of this management concept? What suggestions will you make to your manager to resolve these challenges?

86. If you are employed in a hotel, prepare an outline, similar to that in Figure 11-6, of the guest service cycle at your place of employment.

87. What are "moments of truth"? How can a front office manager identify them?

88. Why must an employee "buy in" to a service management program? What would you do to ensure employee commitment?

89. Discuss some techniques that are useful in determining whether prospective employees have the attributes needed to extend hospitality.

90. Why is training an important component of the service management program? How could a front office manager begin to identify the skills needed for delivery of hospitality? If you are employed in a hotel, did you receive training in delivering hospitality?

91. How can a front office manager measure the effectiveness of a service management program?

92. Why is follow-through so necessary in the continued delivery of hospitality?

## *Situation Handling Skills and SPOs*

### *Situation handling:*

### Skippers:

Skippers often comes with little luggage or no luggage. The bell boys have to be alert to notify the front office about guests with scanty baggage in-order to take necessary advance from them and at the time of check-out.

**How to Prevent Skippers?**

Make sure you always ask guests to fill in registration cards with all details upon check in.

Preauthorize guests credit cards included deposit of a set amount.

On PMS activate a NO post on reservation to stop any extra charges from other outlets to be charged to the guest room.

**Scanty Baggage:**

A guest who checks in to the hotel with very less or no luggage. Scanty baggage means no baggage or a piece of light baggage consisting of briefcase or airbag.

Guest with scanty baggage is normal skippers from the hotel. Skippers are those persons who check out of the hotel without settling their bills. The scanty baggage guests also normally go out with their light baggage and the hotel never knows that if this guest is going out with an intention to come back or not. To save guard the hotels interest, normally guest with scanty baggage are requested to pay in advance.

There is a set procedure adopted by hotels to keep control of guests, with scanty baggage.

- Lobby manager and the reception are notified immediately on guest's arrival about the scanty baggage.
- Arrival errand card is stamped with scanty baggage.
- Guest registration card's all copies are stamped with 'scanty baggage'.
- The scanty baggage register is filled up by the bell desk.
- Get the guest registration cards and the scanty baggage register signed by the lobby manager.

**Walkin Guest:**

A Guest who arrives at a hotel without a reservation is called as 'Walk in'.

The Classic nightmare for any traveller who travel for miles and miles who then walk-in to the hotels and find that the hotel is fully occupied. Hotels have no obligations to accommodate guests who arrive without reservation when no rooms are available for the night.

When the hotel cannot accommodated a walk-in guest, the front office agent can make the situation a little easy for the guest by suggesting and providing directions to alternative hotels nearby.

The front office staff can even call other similar hotels and help the guest to make reservation.

If there seems to be no alternative to turning away the guest, a manager not a front desk agent, should explain the matter in a private office.

Registering one guest in view of another who cannot be accommodated can be extremely awkward and embarrassing.

**Following steps to be clarified before accepting a Walk-in Reservation:**

1. If the guest Presents a confirmation letter, verify the date and the name of the hotel; the guest may have arrived on a different date ir at the wrong hotel.

2. Check with the guest if the reservation was made by another person, it is possible that the reservation agent might have entered the reservation under the booker / caller name!

3. Re verify the reservation by searching the hotel software by last name, first name, reservation number, partial name search, mobile number, Booker name, company, travel agent, etc. If the guest had booked from the travel agent ask the guest to call up the travel agent and get more details of the booking.

4. Ask the guest to reconfirm the arrival date and departure date again, the guest may be arriving on a different date or it is possible that this guest was a no-show for the previous night.

5. If all of the above checks and given negative result then after checking the availability of rooms in the hotel the front desk agent can create a new reservation. When the reservation is created for walk-in guest the source segment of the reservation should be tagged as 'Walk-In'.

6. It is also a good practice to collect a advance deposit for the complete room rental and approximate incidental charges from a Walk-in guest.

**GUEST MESSAGE HANDLING:**

When there is a telephone call or visitor for a resident guest and the guest is not present in the hotel, the front desk agent takes the message for the guest and delivers the same as soon as the guest comes back. The process of receiving and delivering messages to resident guest is known as message handling.

MESSAGE HANDLING PROCEDURE:

1. When there is a visitor or a telephone call for a guest, the front desk assistant should look at the information rack /computer to see whether the guest is a resident guest, future guest or checked-out guest.

2. In case of a resident guest, the agent should check whether the guest is present in the room or not. If the guest is not present in the room, the

agent must check the key rack for the location form. If the same is found act according to the instructions of the guest.

3. If the guest has not left any location form, the front desk assistant should take down the message for the guest on a message slip.

4. The message slip is prepared in duplicate. One copy is placed in the key rack and the second copy is placed in a message slip envelope and slipped through the door of the guest room by the Bell Boy.

5. If there is a visitor or a call for the guest who has checked-out of the hotel, then the front office agent should give information as per the instructions left by the guest.

6. If there is a call for a future guest, then the agent should send the message slip to the back office, where it will be placed along with the reservation record. On the date of arrival of the guest the message slip would be attached to the GRC .so that it can be delivered to the guest at the time of check-in.

7. In some hotels the telephone in the guest room has a message indicator which is switched on to inform the guest that there is a message for him. In some hotels the guest can read the message on the TV in the room.

**PAGING OF GUEST:**

Paging a guest means to locate a guest within the hotel. During their stay guest may be expecting a visitor or an important phone call while he is not in the room. So, in this situation while leaving the guest fills up a form called location form and hand it over to the reception staff. The reception staff should inform the same to the telephone operator. Such that any call for the guest or any visitor for the guest comes we can contact him based on the information on the location form.

Paging is generally done in three methods: - By Page board system: - In front office assistant writes the name of the guest on both sides of the page board and ask the bell boy to locate the guest in the place mentioned on the location form and once the guest is located the message is conveyed to the guest.

By Pager/Beeper System: - In this system the generally the guest is provided with a pager / a beeper and when there is a call or a visitor arrives for the guest the information is sent by the pager at information section and thus guest can contact to the reception. This is generally used in resort hotels where the public area is large.

**HANDLING GUEST ROOM CHANGE:**

Guest rooms are the most important commodity of a hotel. They form a large component of the guests over all experience at a hotel. In case a room doesn't match the guest's expectations, the guest may want to change room. There are times when the hotel may wish to change the room of a resident guest.

A guest may want to change his room for the following reasons:

- If the room assigned is not as per his choice.
- If one or more equipment's in the room are not working satisfactorily.
- If the number of occupants in the room changes.

The hotel may wish to change the guest's room for the following reasons:

- If the requested category of room is not available.
- If the guest overstays and the hotel does not have a room of the same type to allot to the next guest.
- If the room requires maintenance work.

**PROCEDURE FOR CHANGING THE GUEST ROOM:**

Any change in guest room, the front office agent should seek authorization from the Lobby Manager. Front office informs the guest about the room change in advance so that the guest packs his luggage properly. The front office agent fills six copies of room change slip-for reception, bell captain, front desk cashier, telephone exchange, housekeeping and room service-and takes authorization. A bell boy is called and given the keys of the new room. He proceeds to the guest room to shift the guest's luggage. If the change of room is done in the presence of the guest, it is called live move, and if it is carried out in the absence of the guest it is known as dead move. The bellboy collects the room key of the old room and deposits it at the front desk.

**LEFT LUGGAGE:**

The term "Left luggage" is attributed to luggage left by a guest who checks out of the hotel but wishes to collect the luggage later. Guest who wants to visit other cities in a country on a short tour may find. It in convenient tour carries their entire package with them or may find it once economical to retain room in the hotel where they can keep their luggage. Hotel provided the left luggage facilities to guest who are likely to checking to the hotel after they return from the tour. This is not strictly necessary.

Their might be guests who check out but ended to depend much later in the day the occupied they time sight-seeing he would find inconvenient cart their luggage with them. Leave their luggage in the hotel premises under the guarantee by the management luggage would be safe. Some may be charge fees for the facilities. But most of the hotels don't charge the facility. Guest baggage kept in custody of the hotel after the guest has checked out which will be later collected by the guest. The left luggage room is in close proximity to the bell desk where it has racks along the wall where the luggage is deposited. The procedure for handling left luggage is done by the Bell Captain who enters the details in the Left Luggage Register.

Procedure for Left Luggage Handling:

Hotels normally follow the following procedure while accepting the luggage to be stored in the left luggage room:

- The agent makes sure that the guest wishing to keep his luggage in the left luggage room has cleared his bills.
- The luggage tag is filled and tied to each luggage.
- The details of the luggage are entered in the left luggage register.
- The counterfoil of the luggage tag is torn and handed over to the guest.
- The guest is required to present the same for the collection of his luggage.
- The luggage is kept in the left luggage room.

While delivering the luggage to the guest, the following procedure is followed:

- The front office agent requests the guest is to show the luggage tag counterfoil.
- The front office agent tallies the counterfoil with the tag attached to the baggage.
- The front office agent makes an entry in the left luggage register and requests the guest to sign for the delivery of the luggage.
- The front office agent hands over the luggage to the guest.

## *Handling Unusual Events:*

**Terrorist activities and Bomb threat:**

A lodging property that caters the VIPs may face the possible threat of terrorist activity and bomb threat. The hotel should take these threats seriously. The hotel in such situation should liaise with the local police authority and follow the instruction from them. The bomb threat may come by telephone. The person receiving such call should follow the below mentioned points:

- Do not interrupt the caller
- Write the exact words of the caller

<u>If possible find out :</u>

- Time due to explode
- Where the device is placed
- Description of device
- Why he has done it
- Whom they represents
- Write everything as soon as call is disconnected (a bomb threat form may be used for the same if used in hotel) such as: Callers voice, Mannerism, Determination, Age and sex, Accent, Any background noise etc.
- Do not alter the exact talk that has occurred between you and caller while re-telling to the authorities.
- Inform the competent authority immediately.
- Do not spread the rumors.
- Do not attempt to diffuse device if you are able to locate the same.

**Robbery:**

Robbery is a possibility in hotel as there may be a large sum at the front desk cash and bills sections and also at the point of sales. In an event of armed robbery hotel employees should normally follows the below mentioned procedures:

- Comply with the robbers demand
- Do not make sudden movement to provoke the robbers to use weapons or fire arms.
- Remain quiet unless directed to talk by robbers

- Do not attempt to disarm the robber, as this may jeopardize the life of person doing the act and other people in the vicinity.
- The cashier may switch the secret alarm that might be installed in the cash drawer while following the direction of robbers without being suspicious to be noticed by them.
- Observe the person carefully noting the physical characteristics like height, built, eye colour, hair colour, mannerism, complexion, clothing, scar marks or any thing that can be helpful to identification of the robbers.
- The employees may also note the direction of escape, type and registration number of vehicle used by the robbers.
- The employees should refrain themselves for touching any objects that might be touched by the robbers and restrict the movement of the people in the area so that the possible evidences are saved till the policemen comes to the premises.
- The hotel may have a format to record the details of the robber that is gathered from the people who have witnessed the event.

**Death of an In-House Guest in the Hotel:**

Whenever information comes regarding the death of an in-house guest the Front Office Manager should be reported directly who informs the General Manager and the Security Manager. Later on, the police authority is even told and the hotel doctor is summoned to confirm the death of the guest. The residential address of the guests is also identified and the relatives are informed. Once the doctor has confirmed the death and the police have given the permission the dead body is removed by the help of a stretcher. In the meanwhile, if the deceased guest was under some other doctor consultation then that doctor is also enquired.

A death certificate is also prepared and a report is prepared to mention the time, room number and other details related to the deceased guest. The guest room is locked and sealed and after the permission and clearance of police the room is opened and spring cleaned and can be resold again after the approval of the local authority.

**Accident Emergency Situation:**

Accidents can take place in the hotels at any point of time due to faulty stairs, ramps, and balconies and even due to the parking places. The hotels should ensure that handrails, the nonslip surface should be used while framing the architecture plan for the hotels.

**Lost and found:**

This is a term used in hotel parlance to refer to any item which is left by the guest or temporarily misplaced by the guest but traced later by the hotel staff. Such articles to be handed over to the housekeeping department which maintained a special locker for this purpose. If the item belongs to the guest who has already checked out, then a letter has to be sent to the forwarding address left by the guest while checkout or which is there in the registration card. If no reply is received by the hotel within a certain time limit, that may be auctioned to the hotel employees or take a decision as per the hotel policies and rules.

**Illness and Epidemics Emergency Situation:**

There should always be a Doctor on call available for the hotel so that in case if any guest suffers from any kind of problem, he /she can be given the concern treatment as soon as possible.

**Vandalism:**

The front office staff must call the hotel security and order the main door to be locked. If the situation gets out of the hand then the security manager should call the police immediately.

**Damage to property by the resident guest:**

The front office cashier is instructed to raise a charge for the value of the damages to property, a responsible guest will never argue but if he does the subject to be referred to the general manager.

**Handling Drunken Guest:**

A drunken guest may disturb another guest. In order to avoid this, the drunken guest should be escorted to an isolated area like a back office. Hotel staff should calmly handle the situation by following the SOP for handling drunken guests.

**<u>GUEST COMPLAINTS:</u>**

Guest Complaints When guests are not satisfied with some services and express their discontent to hotel employees, most often to the front desk staff, their grievances are recorded as guest complaints.

The guests' complaints can be grouped into four major categories:
- Mechanical
- Attitudinal
- Service-related
- Unusual complaints.

**Mechanical complaints** are related to the malfunctioning or non-functioning of systems and equipment's installed in guest rooms, like television, mini-bar, weather control, channelled music, geyser, and so on.

**Attitudinal Complaint:** When a guest feels insulted by the rude or tactless hotel staff and lodges a complaint, it is referred to as attitudinal complaint. A guest may also make attitudinal complaints when the hotel staffs bother him with their problems.

**Service-related complaints** are about the problems in services provided by the hotel, like delay in the room service of lunch, or delay in the clearance of soiled crockery from the room after meals, etc.

**Unusual complaints** are those over which the hotel does not have any control. For example, a guest may complain about the lack of golf course in the hotel, or the lack of central heating facility, etc. The front office should handle guests' complaints tactfully, exercising patience, empathy, and decision-making skills.

As hospitality is a service-oriented industry, the hotel staff should always try to resolve the customer's problems immediately and thus appease him. If a front office agent is unable to handle a guest's complaint, she should call her superior before the situation gets out of control or becomes worse.

**<u>The following guidelines may be followed while handling guest complaints:</u>**

- Listen silently without interruption, with empathy.
- Show concern and take complaints seriously.
- Never argue. Remember the guest is always right.
- Never try to win an argument you may win the argument but lose the guest forever.
- If possible, isolate the guest so that other guests may not overhear.
- Offer choices and never make a false promise.
- Monitor the corrective measures.
- Follow up and inform the guest about the solution.
- If unable to resolve the guest problem, consult your superiors.
- Address guests by name all communication should be in the first person.
- Use "I am sorry" not "we.
- Don't be defensive. Be composed at all times. Don't take criticisms personally.
- Offer an apology even if the dis-service is not your fault.
- Show empathy by using such phrases as: "I can understand how you feel", "I appreciate what you're saying."
- Tell them what you can do...not what you can't do.

- Find out what it will take to turn their dissatisfaction into satisfaction If they agree to that solution, act quickly before they change their mind.
- Follow-up and inform the guest about the solution.
- If unable to resolve the guest problem, consult your superiors.

# *FRONT OFFICE GLOSSARY*

- **ACCOUNT AGING:-**A method for tracking past due accounts according to the date the charges originated.
- **AGEING STATEMENT: -**A statement which shows how old the unpaid account has become.
- **ACCOUNTANCY CYCLE:-**A period from when a financial transaction occurs to the time it is reconciled and is shown on the financial report of the company.
- **ALLOWANCE:-**The amount which is reduced from the folio as an adjustment against improper, unsatisfactory or no service to the guest. It may also because of posting error.
- **AUDIT TRAIL:-**It is documented history of transactions.
- **BACK OFFICE:-**It is also called as Back Of the House. It is branch of front office department which is responsible for all managerial activities and maintaining ongoing status of the business of the hotel.
- **BAG PULL:-**The process of bringing down the luggage of the group members from their rooms to lobby on the day of departure of the group just before the departure.
- **BLANKET RESERVATION:-**A block of rooms held for a particular group with individual members requesting assignments from that block i.e. a unit that has been reserved for a specific arrival date but not for specific guest, sometimes also referred as blocked room.
- **BLOCK:-** An agreed upon number of rooms set aside for members of group planning to stay at hotel.
- **BOUNCED RESERVATION:-** Sometimes due to some error in planning a guest with reservation may be refused accommodation. This situation is called as bounced reservation. They are also called as Walking of the guest.

- **<u>BUCKET:-</u>**it is specially designed collapsible rack which is normally kept on the cashier's counter top for holding the guest folio. It is also called as <u>cashier's well</u>or <u>folio tray</u>or <u>Tub</u>.
- **<u>BUMPED RESERVATION:-</u>**Refusal of accommodation to a guest holding confirmed reservation and subsequently putting him in some other hotel.
- **<u>CALL ACCOUNTING SYSTEM:-</u>**A device linked to the hotel telephone system that accurately accounts for guest telephone calls by identifying each phone number dialed from guest room telephones and tracking charges.
- **<u>CARD KEY:-</u>**An electronic or magnetic small plastic card used in electronic locking system that operates through a master control console at front desk which is wired to every guest room door. They are also called as <u>magnetic</u>or <u>electronic card</u>.
- **<u>CASH BANK: -</u>**An amount of money given to a cashier at the start of work shift so that he or she can handle the various transactions that occur.
- **<u>CHARGE BACK:-</u>**Sometimes the credit card company refuses the payment of voucher signed by the customer which is sent by the hotel. The given situation is called as charge back.
- **<u>CITY ACCOUNT:-</u>**A non guest account is called as City account.
- **<u>CORKAGE:-</u>**It refers to the charges made by a licensed establishment for providing service equipments, bottle openers, soda etc. to customers who bring their own alcoholic beverage for consumption in the hotel.
- **<u>CUT-OFF-DATE:-</u>**The date by which the confirmations should come otherwise after this date the block of these rooms are released for general sale.
- **<u>DELINQUENT ACCOUNT:-</u>**A city ledger account that has not been settled within a reasonable collection period, usually 90 days.
- **<u>DEMI PENSION:-</u>**Other name of this MAP, <u>Modified American Plan</u>. They are also called as <u>half Pension</u>. In this system room tariff includes Room rent, English breakfast and one major meal i.e. either lunch or dinner.
- **<u>DENIAL CODE:-</u>**A code generated by an online credit card verification service, indicating that the requested transaction has not been approved.
- **<u>DOUBLE UP:-</u>**when a room is occupied by two unrelated guests, it is called as double up.

- **DOWNGRADE:-**Moving the guest's reservation to a lower quality room is called as downgrade.
- **DUE OUT:-**Guests expected to check out on a given day who have not yet done so.
- **DUE BACK:-**A situation that occurs when a cashier pays out more than he or she receives, the difference is due back to cashiers cash bank.
- **EARLY BIRD:-**A term used in fully automatic system of Night Auditing and referring to mainly creating and distribution of reports. It is also called as <u>Flash</u>.
- **END OF THE DAY:-**An arbitrary stopping point for the business day.
- **EXPRESS CHECK OUT:-**A pre departure activity that involves the production and early morning distribution of guest folios for guests expected to check out that morning.
- **FLEX TIME:-**A program of flexible work hours that allows employees to vary their times of starting and ending work.
- **FLOOR LIMIT:-**A limit assigned to hotels by credit card companies indicating the maximum amount in credit card charges the hotel is permitted to accept from a card member without special authorization.
- **FOLIO:-** A statement of all transactions affecting the balance of single account.
- **FORFEITED DEPOSIT:-**The amount that the guest has paid as advance for booking a room, may be forfeited whole or some in case of his no-show and is called as <u>Retention charge</u>in that case.
- **FRANKING MACHINE:-**A machine which is used for printing postage stamp value on the envelope.
- **FRONT OF THE HOUSE:-** those part of front office department with which the guest come in direct contact.
- **FULL DAY:-** It is way of measuring a chargeable day for accounting purpose for a guest. For example it will be three meals for an American plan hotel and no meals and only overnight stay for European hotels.
- **GARNI HOTELS:-**A hotel which has no food and beverage service facility.
- **GLOBAL DISTRIBUTION SYSTEM:-**A distribution channel for reservations that provides worldwide distribution of hotel reservation information and allows the selling of hotel reservations around the world, usually accomplished by connecting the hotel company reservation system with an airline reservation system.
- **GRAVEYARD SHIFT:-**A work shift which begins from midnight.

- **GATEWAY CITY:-**A city located in an area that makes them the first practical stop for an International Flight Coming in to a country.
- **HOUSE COUNT:-** Total number of guest is staying in the hotel at a particular time.
- **HOUSE LIMIT:-**A credit limit established by hotel.
- **HUBBART FORMULA:-**A formulae developed by Ray Hubbart for determining room rate keeping in consideration operating expenses, room sales, and pre desired return on investment (ROI).
- **HURDLE RATE:-**The minimum retail price below which the room cannot be sold.
- **IDLE TIME:-**it is also called as <u>hidden rest</u>. This is period that must be allowed during duty when a person does not work.
- **IN BALANCE:-**A term describing the state of accounts when the totals of debit amounts and credit amounts are equal.
- **INCIDENTAL ACCOUNT:-**Charges which are guest's own responsibility, which is not paid by the company or tour operators.
- **INTER SELL AGENCY:-**A reservation system that handles reservation for many products such as airlines, car rentals and hotels etc.
- **KEY CARD:-**Sometimes used as identification card given to a guest, but usually contains general information facility, catering outlets, location of the hotel etc., which is given by the receptionist at the time of check in.
- **KEYING:-**Coding system used in an advertisement to identify the response from the media.
- **LATE CHECK OUT:-**A guest who with the permission of the hotel checks out of the hotel after the check out time, without paying any extra charge.
- **LATE CHARGES:-**The amount of any purchase informed by any point of sale cashier to the main cashier after the departure of guest and which remains outstanding.
- They are also the charges which hotel imposes to a guest who does not leave at check out time and wants to stay for few extra hours.
- **LEAD TIME:-**The time between when a reservation is made and when the guest is due to arrive.
- **LEDGER:-** A grouping of accounts.
- **LOCK OUT:-**When a guest is not allowed access to the room usually due to an unpaid bill.
- **MARKET MIX:-**The distribution in percentage of the hotel guest into various categories such as tourist, businessman etc.

- **NET CASH RECEIPT:-**The amount of cash and checks in the cashier's drawer minus the amount of initial cash bank.
- **NO- SHOW:-**A guest who made a room reservation but did not register or cancel.
- **OFF:-**It means that the room is off the list of rooms available for sale due to some reason. Also called as <u>Red Slip Room</u>.
- **OPTION DATE:-**It is the designated date by which the prospective guest is required to confirm his booking.
- **OUT OF BALANCE:-**A term used to describe the state of accounts when the totals of debit amounts and credit amounts do not equal.
- **OVERAGE:-**An imbalance that occurs when the total of cash and checks in cash register drawer is greater than the initial cash bank plus net cash receipts.
- **OVERBOOKING:-**A situation in which hotel books more room than available.
- **OVERDUE ACCOUNT:-**A city ledger account that is unpaid beyond the current billing period, usually between 30 and 90 days.
- **OVERFLOW FACILITY:-**A property selected to receive central system reservation requests after room availabilities in the system's participating properties within a geographic region has been exhausted.
- **OVERSTAY GUEST:-**A Guest who stays after his or her stated departure date.
- **PAID IN ADVANCE:-**A guest who pays his or her room charges in cash during registration. PIA guests are often denied in house credit facility.
- **PAIDOUT:-**Cash disbursed by the hotel on behalf of a guest and charged to the guest's account as a cash advance.
- **PRODUCT LIFE CYCLE:-**It is a concept which says that all products have a point of growth, maturity and decline due to change and competition.
- **RACK RATE:-** The maximum retail price of the room is called as Rack Rate.
- **RACK SLIP:-**A paper slip which is adjusted in racks such as reservation rack, room rack and information rack.
- **RATE CUTTING:-**Reducing room tariff to attract more business.
- **RED BOOK:-**A hard bound register used in diary system in non automated method of registration.
- **RELEASE DATE:-**Rooms may be allocated to agents for sale who may deal with them without reference to the hotel. The release date is the point at which the control of the sale rests to the hotel. Usually 24 to 48

hours before each sale date.

- **RETENTION CHARGE:-**These are the charges which may be collected from guest for making guaranteed reservation in the hotel and when does not turn up on the scheduled date due to reasons best known to him.
- **ROUTING:-**The process where credits/debits incurred by one account are manually or automatically transferred to another account.
- **ROOM COUNT:-**The number of occupied rooms in a hotel.
- **ROOMING:-**A procedure of escorting the guest and carrying of his luggage to the assigned room by the bell boy.
- **RUN OF THE HOUSE:-**Room assignment based on room availability at the time of check in.
- **SEAMLESS CONNECTIVITY:-**the ability of travel agencies to book reservations directly into hotel reservation systems as well as verify room availability and rates.
- **SHOULDER PERIOD:-**A mid price season between peak and off season.
- **SHORTAGE:-**an imbalance that occurs when the total of cash and checks in a cash register drawer is less than the initial bank plus net cash receipts.
- **SIBERIA:-**A term normally used for inferior quality rooms , such as near the staircase etc. guest must be informed about its situation and condition before selling it.
- **SKIPPER:-**A guest who leaves the hotel without settling his bill.
- **SLEEP OUT:-**A sold room where the guest did not stay during the night.
- **SLEEPER:-**Room available for sale but not sold out.
- **SLIPPAGE:-**The term used when analyzing the group room performance. It is difference between what is contracted and what actually arrives.
- **SPLIT FOLIO:-**Folio in which guest's charges is separated into two or more folios.
- **STAY OVER:-**A room status term indicates that the guest is not checking out today and will remain at least one more night.
- **STOP OVER GUEST:-**They are also called as <u>layover guest</u>. This refers to the guest who en route from one destination to another stops in between on a third destination and breaks his journey. This is generally on airlines expenses.
- **SUPPLEMENTAL TRANSCRIPT:-**A detailed report of all non guests account that indicates each charge transaction that affected a non guest account that day, used as a worksheet to detect posting errors.

- **TRAFFIC SHEET:-**A telephone department control sheet usually used for long distance calls.
- **TRANSPOSITION ERROR:-**also called as transcription error and is caused by wrong recording of sequence of digits for example 289 is written as 298.
- **TURN AWAY:-**To refuse accommodation to walk in guest, because the rooms are not available. They are also called as <u>Displacement</u>.
- **TURN DOWN:-**An evening service provided by housekeeper where she prepares the bed for night use.
- **TURN IN:-**The cash deposited by the departmental cashier with general cashier at the end of the day.
- **TIPSY GUEST:-**A drunkard guest who may misbehave with the staff.
- **UNDER BOOKING:-**An erroneous belief that all the rooms are sold while in fact they are not.
- **UNDERSTAY:-**A guest who checks out before his scheduled date of departure.
- **VPO: -**Visitors Paid Out. If small Payments are made by front desk on the behalf of guest such as taxi fare, cinema tickets etc., then a voucher is prepared called as Visitors paid out voucher which is signed by guest and later settled at the time of departure.
- **VOUCHER:-**The signed bills of the guest which is settled at the time of departure of the guest.
- **WALK OUT:-**A skipper guest is also called as walk out guest.
- **WALK IN:-**A guest who comes to the hotel without prior reservation. They are also called as <u>Chance guest</u>or <u>Off Street Guest</u>.
- **WALKING:-**Due to lack of availability of rooms, once the accommodation is refused to a guest who is holding reservation are called as Walking of the guest. They are also called as <u>Bounced Reservation.</u>
- **WASH FACTOR:-**Deletions of unnecessary group rooms from a group block.
- **WATCH DOWN:-**Blocking fewer rooms than the number requested by the group, based on group history.
- **WHO:-**An unidentified guest in a room that is vacant as per front desk record.
- **YIELD:-**The ratio actual rooms revenue to the potential room revenue.
- **ZEROING OUT:-**At the time of departure bringing the account balance to zero.

# FRONT OFFICE ABBREVIATIONS

- AHMA - American Hotel & Motel Association
- AH&LA – American Hotel & Lodging Association
- AH&LEI – American hotel & lodging Educational Institute
- A.M - Antemeridian
- CCTV - Closed Circuit Tele Vision
- CVGR - Company Volume Guaranteed Rate
- CIP - Commercially Important Person
- DG - Distinguished Guest
- DNA - Did Not Arrive
- DND – Do Not Disturb
- DNS - Did Not Stay
- DSS - Decision Support system
- ECO - Express Check Out
- EDC - Electronic Data Capturing
- EDP - Electronic Data Processing
- EPBX - Electronic Private Branch Exchange
- EPABX - Electronic Private Automatic Branch Exchange
- FERA - Foreign Exchange Regulation Act
- FIT - Free Individual Traveller/ Free independent traveller
- FFIT - Foreign Free Independent Traveller
- FHRAI - Federation of Hotels & Restaurant Association Of India
- FF&E - Furniture, Fixture & Equipment
- FRRO - Foreigner's Regional Registration Office
- GDS - Global Distribution System
- GIT - Group Inclusive Tour
- HIS - Hotel Information System
- HAI - Hotel Association of India
- HLP - Heat Light & Power
- HRACC - Hotel & Restaurant Approval & Classification Committee
- IATA - International Air Transport Association
- IATO - Indian Association of Tour Operation
- IHRA - International Hotel & restaurant Associates

- ISD - International Subscribers Dialling
- MAP - Modified American plan
- MCO - Miscellaneous Charge
- MIS - Management Information System
- MLS - Minimum Length of Stay
- MOD - Managers on Duty
- NTA - Not to be allotted
- OOO - Out of order
- PPPN - per person per night
- PIA - Paid in advance
- PRPN - Per room per night
- POS - Point of Sale
- PSO - Passengers service order
- RNA - Room not assigned
- SITS - Special Interest Tours
- STD - Subscriber Trunk Dialling
- SOP - Standard Operating Procedures
- SPATT - Special Attention Guest
- TQM - Total Quality Management
- TAAI - Travel Agents Association of India
- UFTAA - Universal Federation of Travel Agent Association
- VIP - Very Important Person
- VPO - Visitors Paid Out
- VR - Vacant & Ready
- WATS - Wide Area Telephone Services
- WTO - World Travel Organization
- WATA - World Association of Travel Agents.

## Glossary for Campus Placements and Job Interviews in FRONT OFFICE:

- **access time:** the amount of time required for a processor to retrieve information from the hard drive; recorded in milliseconds

- **accounts payable:** financial obligations the hotel owes to private and government-related agencies and vendors
- **accounts receivable:** amounts of money owed to the hotel by guests **aging of accounts:** indication of the stage of the payment cycle—such as 10 days old, 30 days overdue, 60 days overdue
- **all-suites:** a level of service provided by a hotel for a guest who will desire a more at home atmosphere
- **amenities:** personal toiletry items such as shampoo, toothpaste, mouthwash, and electrical equipment
- **American Hotel & Lodging Association:** a professional association of hotel owners, managers, and related occupations
- **American plan:** a room rate that includes meals, usually breakfast and the evening meal, as well as room rental in the room rate
- **Americans with Disabilities Act (ADA):** a U.S. law enacted in 1990 that protects people with disabilities from being discriminated against when seeking accommodations and employment
- **assets:** items that have monetary value
- **assistant general manager:** a person in the hotel who executes plans developed by the corporate owners, general manager, and other members of the management staff
- **athletics director:** the person responsible for supervising physical exercise facilities for guests
- **atrium concept:** a design in which guest rooms overlook the lobby from the first floor to the roof
- **average daily rate (ADR):** a measure of the hotel staff's ability to sell available room rates;
- the method to compute the ADR is: room revenue / number of rooms sold
- **back office:** the accounting office of a hotel
- **back office accounts payable:** amounts of money that have been prepaid on behalf of the guest for future consumption of a good or service (sometimes referred to as back office cash accounts)
- **balance sheet:** an official financial listing of assets, liabilities, and owner's equity
- **bank cards:** credit cards issued by banks, examples of which include Visa, MasterCard, and JCB
- **banquet manager:** a person who is responsible for fulfilling the details of service for a banquet or special event

- **banquet sheet:** a listing of the details of an event at which food and beverages are served
- **bell captain:** the supervisor of the bell staff
- **bell staff:** people who lift and tote baggage, familiarize guests with their new surroundings, run errands, deliver supplies, provide guests with information on in-house marketing efforts and local attractions, and act as the hospitality link between the lodging establishment and the guest
- **bill-to-account:** an extension of credit to a guest by an individual hotel, which requires the guest or the guest's employer to establish a line of credit and to adhere to a regular payment schedule
- **blackout:** total loss of electricity
- **blocking on the horizon:** reserving guest rooms in the distant future
- **blocking procedure:** process of reserving a room on a specific day
- **bottom up:** a sales method that involves presenting the least expensive rate first
- **brownouts:** partial loss of electricity
- **bus association network:** an organization of bus tour owners and operators who offer transportation and travel information to groups
- **business affiliations:** chain or independent ownership of hotels
- **business services and communications centre:** guest services that include copying, computers, fax, etc.
- **call accounting:** a computerized system that allows for automatic tracking and posting of outgoing guest room calls
- **cancellation code:** a sequential series of alphanumeric combinations that provide the guest with a reference for a cancellation of a guaranteed reservation
- **cash bank:** a specific amount of paper money and coins issued to a cashier to be used for making change
- **cashier:** a person who processes guest checkouts and guest legal tender and makes change for guests
- **cashier's report:** a daily cash control report that lists cashier activity of cash and credit cards and machine totals by cashier shift
- **chain:** a group of hotels that follow standard operating procedures such as marketing, reservations, quality of service, food and beverage operations, housekeeping, and accounting
- **chain affiliations:** hotels that purchase operational and marketing services from a corporation

- **city ledger accounts:** a collection of accounts receivable of nonregistered guests who use the services of the hotel
- **collective bargaining unit:** a labour union
- **commercial cards:** credit cards issued by corporations, an example of which is Diners Club
- **commercial hotels:** hotels that provide short-term accommodations for travelling guests
- **commercial rates:** room rates for businesspeople who represent a company but do not necessarily have less bargaining power because of their infrequent or sporadic pattern of travel
- **communications hierarchy:** a listing of the order in which management personnel may be called on to take charge in an emergency situation
- **company-owned property:** a hotel that is owned and operated by a chain organization
- **complimentary rate (comp):** a rate for which there is no charge to the guest
- **computer supplies:** paper, forms, ribbons, ink cartridges, and floppy disks needed to operate the system
- **concierge:** a person who provides an endless array of information on entertainment, sports, amusements, transportation, tours, church services, and baby-sitting in a particular city or town
- **conference call:** a conversation in which three or more persons are linked by telephone
- **confirmed reservations:** prospective guests who have a reservation for accommodations that is honoured until a specified time
- **continental breakfast:** juice, fruit, sweet roll, and/or cereal
- **controller:** the internal accountant for the hotel
- **convention guests:** guests who attend a large convention and receive a special room rate
- **corporate client:** a hotel guest who represents a business or is a guest of that business and provides the hotel with an opportunity to establish a regular flow of business during sales periods that would normally be flat
- **corporate guests:** frequent guests who are employed by a company and receive a special room rate
- **corporate rates:** room rates offered to corporate clients staying in the hotel
- **CPS (characters per second):** measure of the speed with which individual characters are printed

- **credit:** a decrease in an asset or an increase in a liability, or an amount of money the hotel owes the guest
- **credit balance:** amounts of money a hotel owes guests in future services
- **credit-card imprinter:** makes an imprint of the credit card the guest will use as the method of payment
- **credit-card validator:** a computer terminal linked to a credit-card data bank that holds information concerning the customer's current balance and security status
- **crisis management:** maintaining control of an emergency situation
- **cross-training:** training employees for performing multiple tasks and jobs
- **cumulative total feature:** an electronic feature of a PMS that adds all posted room rate amounts previously entered into one grand total
- **current guests:** guests who are registered in the hotel
- **cursor:** a flashing point on a monitor that indicates where data can be entered on a computer screen
- **cycle of service:** the progression of a guest's request for products and services through a hotel's departments
- **daily announcement board:** an inside listing of the daily activities of the hotel (time, group, and room assignment)
- **daily blocking:** assigning guests to their particular rooms on a daily basis
- **daily flash report:** a PMS listing of departmental totals by day, period to date, and year to date, which helps the manager to determine the financial success of the previous day and the current status in achieving other financial goals
- **daily function sheet:** a listing of the planned events in the hotel
- **daily sales report:** a financial activity report produced by a department in a hotel that reflects daily sales activities with accompanying cash register tapes or point-of-sale audit tapes
- **database interfaces:** the sharing of information among computers
- **data sorts:** report options in a PMS that indicate groupings of information
- **debit:** an increase in an asset or a decrease in a liability
- **debit balance:** an amount of money the guest owes the hotel
- **debit cards:** embossed plastic cards with a magnetic strip on the reverse side that authorize direct transfer of funds from a customer's bank account to the commercial organization's bank account for purchase of goods and services

- **demographic data:** size, density, distribution, vital statistics of a population, broken down into, for example, age, sex, marital status, and occupation categories
- **departmental accounts:** income- and expense-generating areas of the hotel, such as restaurants, gift shop, and banquets
- **desk clerk:** the person who verifies guest reservations, registers guests, assigns rooms, distributes keys, communicates with the housekeeping staff, answers telephones, gives information about and directions to local attractions, accepts cash and gives change, and acts as liaison between the lodging establishment and the guest as well as the community
- **direct-mail letters:** letters sent directly to individuals in a targeted market group in a marketing effort
- **director of marketing and sales:** the person who analyzes available markets, suggests products and services to meet the needs of those markets, and sells these products and services at a profit
- **director of security:** the person who works with department directors to develop procedures that help ensure employee honesty and guest safety
- **discount rate:** a percentage of the total sale that is charged by the credit card agency to the commercial enterprise for the convenience of accepting credit cards
- **discretionary income:** the money remaining from wages after paying for necessities such as food, clothing, and shelter
- **disk drive:** a place in the computer where data is stored or read; hard or floppy—31/2- inch versus 51/4-inch
- **distance learning:** learning that takes place via satellite broadcasts, PictureTel, or on-line computer interaction
- **documentation:** printed or on-screen (monitor) instructions for operating hardware or software that accompany a specific PMS
- **dot-matrix:** a printer that produces small dots printed with an inked ribbon on paper
- **double occupancy percentage:** a measure of a hotel's staff ability to attract more than one guest to a room; the method to compute double occupancy percentage is:
- = {(number of guests - number of rooms sold)/ number of rooms sold} x 100
- **draft-style:** a good type of dot-matrix print
- **eco-tourists:** tourists who plan vacations to understand the culture and environment of a particular area

- **electronic key:** a plastic key with electronic codes embedded on a magnetic strip
- **electronic key system:** a system composed of battery-powered or, less frequently, hardwired locks; a host computer and terminals; a keypuncher; and special entry cards that are used as keys
- **elevator operator:** a person who manually operates the mechanical controls of the elevator
- **E-mail:** a communication system that uses an electronic network to send messages via computers
- **employee handbook:** publication that provides general guidelines concerning employee conduct
- **empowerment:** management's act of delegating certain authority and responsibility to frontline employees
- **ergonomics:** the study of how people relate psychologically and physiologically to machines
- **escort service:** having a uniformed security guard escort a hotel employee to a financial institution
- **euro:** the accepted currency for some European states: Belgium, Germany, Spain, France, Ireland, Italy, Luxembourg, the Netherlands, Austria, Portugal, Finland, and Greece
- **European plan:** a rate that quotes room charges only
- **executive housekeeper:** a person who is responsible for the upkeep of the guest rooms and public areas of the lodging property as well as control of guest room inventory items
- **express checkout:** means by which the guest uses computer technology in a guest room or a computer in the hotel lobby to check out
- **extended stay:** a level of service that attracts long-term guests by providing light food service and amenities that include fully equipped kitchenette, spacious bedrooms, and living areas for relaxation and work
- **FAM (familiarization) tours:** complimentary visits sponsored by the lodging property that host representatives of travel organizations, bus associations, social and non-profit organizations,and local corporate traffic managers
- **family rates:** room rates offered to encourage visits by families with children
- **fax machine:** equipment for facsimile reproduction via telephone lines
- **fire safety display terminal:** a device that ensures a constant surveillance of sprinkler systems and smoke detectors

- **float:** the delay in payment from an account after using a credit card or personal check
- **floor inspector:** a person who supervises the housekeeping function on a floor of a hotel
- **floor limit:** a dollar amount set by the credit-card agency that allows for a maximum amount of guest charges
- **flow analysis processes:** the preparation of a schematic drawing of the operations included in a particular function
- **flowchart:** an analysis of the delivery of a particular product or service
- **folio:** a guest's record of charges and payments
- **folio well:** a device that holds the individual guest folios and city ledger folios
- **food and beverage director:** a person who is responsible for the efficient operation of the kitchen, dining rooms, banquet service, room service, and lounge
- **foot patrol:** walking the halls, corridors, and outside property of a hotel to dctcct breaches of guest and employee safety
- **forecasting:** projecting room sales for a specific period
- **franchisee:** a hotel owner who has access to a national reservation system and receives the benefits of the corporation's management expertise, financial backing, national advertising, and group purchasing
- **frontline employees:** employees who deliver service to guests as front desk clerks, cashiers, switchboard operators, bellhops, concierge, and housekeeping employees
- **front office:** the communication, accounting, and service centre of the hotel
- **front office manager:** the person responsible for leading the front office staff in delivering hospitality
- **full house:** 100 percent hotel occupancy; a hotel that has all its guest rooms occupied
- **full service:** a level of service provided by a hotel with a wide range of conveniences for the guest
- **function sheet:** listing of the daily events in a hotel, such as meetings, etc.
- **general ledger:** a collection of accounts that the controller uses to organize the financial activities of the hotel
- **general manager:** the person in charge of directing and leading the hotel staff in meeting its financial, environmental, and community

responsibilities

- **gigabyte:** 1,024 megabytes of formatted capacity
- **group planner:** the person responsible for securing guest room accommodations, food and beverage programs, transportation reservations, meeting facilities, registration procedures, tours, and information on sightseeing, while maintaining a budget for group travellers
- **group rates:** room rates offered to large groups of people visiting the hotel for a common reason
- **group travellers:** persons who are travelling on business or for pleasure in an organized fashion
- **guaranteed reservations:** prospective guests who have made a contract with the hotel for a guest room
- **guest folio:** a form imprinted with the hotel's logo and a control number and allowing space for room number, guest identification, date in and date out, and room rate in the upper left-hand corner; it allows for guest charges to be imprinted with a PMS and is filed in room-number sequence
- **guest histories:** details concerning the guests' visits, such as zip code, frequency of visits, corporate affiliation, or special needs
- **guest test:** evaluation procedure in which an outside person is hired by the hotel to experience hotel services and report the findings to management
- **half-day rate:** a room rate based on length of guest stay in a room
- **hard key:** a metal device used to trip tumblers in a mechanical lock
- **hard-key system:** a security device consisting of the traditional hard key that fits into a keyhole in a lock; preset tumblers inside the lock are turned by the designated key
- **hardware:** computer equipment used to process software, such as central processing units, keyboards, monitors, and printers
- **hospitality:** the generous and cordial provision of services to a guest
- **Hospitality Television (HTV):** a commercial hospitality educational organization based in Louisville, Kentucky, that provides satellite broadcasts to hotels, restaurants, and food service facilities
- **hotel broker:** a person who sells hotel room prize packages to corporations, sweepstakes promoters, game shows, and other sponsors
- **hotel representative:** a member of the marketing and sales department of the hotel who actively seeks out group activities planners

- **house count:** the number of persons registered in a hotel on a specific night
- **housekeeper's room report:** a daily report that lists the occupancy status of each room according to the housekeeping department
- **housekeeping room status:** terminology that indicates availability of a guest room such as available, clean, or ready (room is ready to be occupied), occupied (guest or guests are already occupying a room), dirty or stay over (guest will not be checking out of a room on the current day), on change (guest has checked out of the room, but the housekeeping staff has not released the room for occupancy), and out-of-order (the room is not available for occupancy because of a mechanical malfunction)
- **house limit:** a dollar amount set by the hotel that allows for a maximum amount of guest charges
- **Hubbart formula:** a method used to compute room rates that considers such factors as operating expenses, desired return on investment, and income from various departments in the hotel
- **human resources manager:** the person responsible for administering federal, state, and local employment laws as well as advertising, screening, interviewing, selecting, orienting, training, and evaluating employees
- **incentive program:** an organized effort by management to understand employees' motivational concerns and develop opportunities for employees to achieve both their goals and the goals of the hotel
- **independent hotel:** a hotel that is not associated with a franchise
- **in-house laundry:** a hotel-operated department that launders linens, uniforms, bedspreads, etc.
- **ink-jet:** a printer that produces small dots printed with liquid ink on paper
- **inquiries/reports:** a feature of the PMS that enables management to maintain a current view of operations and finances
- **in-room guest checkout:** a feature of the property management system that allows the guest to use a guest room television to check out of a hotel
- **in-service education:** courses that update a professional's educational background for use in current practice
- **interdepartmental communication:** communication between departments

- **interfacing:** the ability of computers to communicate electronically and share data
- **interhotel property referrals:** a system in which one member-property recommends another member-property to a guest
- **Internet:** a network of computer systems that share information over high-speed electronic connections
- **inter-sell cards:** credit cards issued by a hotel corporation, similar to private label cards
- **intradepartmental communication:** communication inside a department
- **I/O ports (input/output devices):** keyboards, monitors, modems, mouse, joystick, light pen, printers, and track balls
- **job analysis:** a detailed listing of the tasks performed in a job, which provides the basis for a sound job description
- **job description:** a listing of required duties to be performed by an employee in a particular job
- **keyboard:** a standard or Dvorak-type typewriter-style keypad that allows the operator to enter or retrieve data
- **key clerk:** a person who issues keys to registered guests and other hotel personnel and sorts incoming mail for registered guests and management staff
- **key drawer:** a drawer located underneath the counter of the front desk that holds room keys in slots in numerical order
- **key fob:** a decorative and descriptive plastic or metal tag attached to a hard key
- **keypad:** a numeric collection of typewriter keys and function keys that allows the operator to enter numbers or perform math functions in a computer
- **laser:** a printer that produces photo images on paper
- **late charges:** guest charges that might not be included on the guest folio because of a delay in posting by other departments
- **letter-quality:** a better type of dot-matrix print
- **liabilities:** financial or other contractual obligations or debts
- **limited service:** a level of service provided by a hotel with guest room accommodations and limited food service and meeting space
- **litigious society:** an environment in which consumers sue providers of products and services for not delivering those products and services according to expected operating standards

- **main menu:** on-screen list of all the available individual programs (modules) that are included in the software system
- **maintenance manager:** a staff member in a limited-service property who maintains the heating and air-conditioning plant, produces guest room keys, assists housekeeping attendants as required, and assists with guest safety and security
- **management contract property:** a hotel that is operated by a consulting company that provides operational and marketing expertise and a professional staff
- **manager's report:** a listing of occupancy statistics from the previous day, such as occupancy percentage, yield percentage, average daily rate, RevPAR, and number of guests
- **market segments:** identifiable groups of customers with similar needs for products and services
- **marquee:** the curbside message board, which includes the logo of the hotel and space for a message
- **mass marketing:** advertising products and services through mass communications such as television, radio, and the Internet
- **master credit card account:** an accounts receivable that tracks bank, commercial, private label, and intersell credit cards such as Visa, MasterCard, and JCB
- **megabyte:** 1,024 kilobytes of formatted capacity
- **megahertz(mHz):** one million cycles per second; indicates computer speed
- **message book:** a loose-leaf binder in which the front desk staff on various shifts can record important messages
- **military and educational rates:** room rates established for military personnel and educators
- **modem:** computer hardware that allows for transfer of data through telephone lines, data expressed in baud—information transfer—rates
- **modified American plan:** a room rate that offers one meal with the price of a room rental
- **moments of truth:** every time the hotel guest comes in contact with some aspect of the hotel, he or she judges its hospitality
- **money wire:** an electronic message that authorizes money from one person to be issued to another person
- **monitor:** a television screen with color or monochrome capacity to view input and output data, control column width and line length of display,

adjust height of character display, and allow visual control

- **moonlighter:** a person who holds a full-time job at one organization and a part-time job at another organization
- **motivation:** investigating employee needs and desires and developing a framework for meeting them
- **Murphy bed:** a bed that is hinged at the base of the headboard and swings up into the wall for storage, an example being the SICO brand wall-bed
- **needs analysis:** assessment of the flow of information and services of a specific property to determine if proposed new equipment can improve the flow
- **night audit:** the control process whereby the financial activity of guests' accounts is maintained and balanced on a daily basis
- **night auditor:** a person who balances the daily financial transactions of guests who have used hotel services, acts as a desk clerk for the night shift, and communicates with the controller
- **no-show factor:** percentage of guests with confirmed or guaranteed reservations who do not show up
- **occupancy management formula:** alculation that considers confirmed reservations, guaranteed reservation, no-show factors of these two types of reservations, predicted stay over, predicted under stays, and predicted walk-ins to determine the number of additional room reservations needed to achieve 100 percent occupancy
- **occupancy percentage:** the number of rooms sold divided by the number of rooms available
- **on-line:** operational and connected to the main computer system
- **on-the-job training:** a training process in which the employee observes and practices a task while performing his or her job
- **operational effectiveness:** the ability of a manager to control costs and meet profit goals
- **operational reports:** operational data on critical financial aspects of hotel operations
- **optimal occupancy:** achieving 100 percent occupancy with room sales that will yield the highest room rate
- **optimal room rate:** a room rate that approaches the rack rate
- **organization charts:** schematic drawings that list management positions in an organization

- **orientation checklist:** a summary of all items that must be covered during orientation
- **orientation process:** the introduction of new hires to the organization and work environment, in order to provide background information about the property
- **outsourcing:** provision of service to the hotel—for example, a central reservation system— by an agency outside of the hotel
- **outstanding balance report:** a listing of guests' folio balances
- **overbooking:** accepting reservations for more rooms than are available by forecasting the number of no-show reservations, stayovers, understays, and walk-ins, with the goal of attaining 100 percent occupancy
- **package rate:** room rates that include goods and services in addition to rental of a room
- **paid in advance (PIA):** guests who paid cash at check-in
- **paid-outs:** amounts of monies paid out of the cashier's drawer on behalf of a guest or an employee of the hotel
- **paid-out slips:** prenumbered forms that authorize cash disbursement from the front desk clerk's bank for products on behalf of a guest or an employee of the hotel
- **parking garage manager:** the person responsible for supervising garage attendants and maintaining security of guests and cars in the parking garage
- **payback period:** the period of time required for the hotel to recoup purchase price, installation charges, financing fees, and so forth through cost savings and increased guest satisfaction; assists in deciding whether to install computers
- **Peddler's Club:** a marketing program meant to encourage repeat business by frequent business guests
- **percent occupancy:** the number of rooms sold divided by the number of rooms available multiplied by 100
- **percent yield:** the number of rooms sold at average daily rate versus number of rooms available at rack rate multiplied by 100
- **physical plant engineer:** the person who oversees a team of electricians; plumbers; heating, ventilating, and air-conditioning contractors; and general repair people to provide behindthe-cenes services to the guests and employees of the lodging property

- **Picture Tel:** the use of telephone lines to send and receive video and audio impressions
- **plant:** an outside person who is hired by a hotel to experience hotel services and report the findings to management
- **pleasure travellers:** people who travel alone or with others on their own for visits to points of interest, to relatives, or for other personal reasons
- **point-of-sale:** an outlet in the hotel that generates income, such as a restaurant, gift shop, spa, or garage
- **point-of-sale front office:** a front office whose staff promotes other profit centres of the hotel
- **point-of-sale terminals:** computerized cash registers that interface with a property management system
- **policy and procedure manual:** publication that provides an outline of how the specific duties of each job are to be performed
- **postal code:** *See* zip or postal code
- **posting:** the process of debiting and crediting charges and payments to a guest folio
- **potential gross income:** the amount of sales a hotel might obtain at a given level of occupancy, average daily rate, and anticipated yield
- **ppm (pages per minute):** printing speed capability
- **predicted house count:** an estimate of the number of guests expected to register based on previous occupancy activities
- **printer:** computer hardware in dot-matrix, ink-jet, or laser models that produces hard copies of output data in letter quality or draft style in various print fonts, with printing speed being expressed in CPS (characters per second), number of characters per line, and pages per minute and paper insertion being tractor-fed, single-sheet, or continuous-form
- **prior approved credit:** use of a credit card to establish creditworthiness
- **private label cards:** credit cards issued by a retail organization, such as a department store or gasoline company
- **processor speed:** how fast a CPU (central processing unit) makes calculations per second; expressed in MHz (the abbreviation for "megahertz")
- **profit-and-loss statement:** a listing of revenues and expenses for a certain time period
- **property management system (PMS):** a generic term used to describe applications of computer hardware and software used to manage a hotel

by networking reservation and registration databases, point-of-sale systems, accounting systems, and other office software

- **psychographic data:** emotional and motivational forces that affect a service or product for potential markets
- **rack rate:** the highest room rate category offered by a hotel
- **real estate investment trust (REIT):** a form of financing an investment in real estate through a mutual fund
- **recreation director:** the person who is in charge of developing and organization recreational activities for guests
- **referral member:** a hotel owner or developer who has access to the national reservation system
- **referral property:** a hotel operating as an independent that wishes to be associated with a certain chain; uses national reservation system
- **referral reservation service:** a service offered by a management company of a chain of hotels to franchisee members
- **registration card:** a form on which the guest indicates name, home or billing address, home or billing phone number, vehicle information, date of departure, and method of payment
- **reservation code:** a sequential series of alphanumeric combinations that provide the guest with a reference for a guaranteed reservation
- **reservation referral system:** a worldwide organization that processes requests for room reservations at a particular member-hotel
- **reservations manager:** the person who takes and confirms incoming requests for rooms, noting special requests for service; provides guest with requested information; maintains an accurate room inventory; and communicates with marketing and sales
- **reservation status:** terminology used to indicate the availability of a guest room to be rented on a particular night, i.e., open (room is available for renting), confirmed (room has been reserved until 4:00 p.m. or 6:00 p.m.) guaranteed (room has been reserved until guest arrives), and repair (room is not available for guest rental)
- **residential hotels:** hotels that provide long-term accommodations for guests
- **revenue account:** part of owner's equity
- **revenue per available room (RevPAR):** the amount of dollars each hotel room produces for the overall financial success of the hotel, determined by dividing room revenues received for a specific day by the number of rooms available in the hotel for that day

- **revenue potential:** the room revenue that could be received if all the rooms were sold at the rack rate
- **revenue realized:** the actual amount of room revenue earned (number of rooms sold _actual rate)
- **role-playing:** acting out a role before actually being required to do the job.
- **room attendants:** employees who clean and maintain guest rooms and public areas
- **room blocking:** reserving rooms for guests who are holding reservations
- **room key control system:** an administrative procedure that authorizes certain personnel and registered guests to have access to keys
- **room revenues:** the amount of room sales received
- **room sales figure:** the total of posted daily guest room charges
- **room sales projections:** a weekly report prepared and distributed by the front office manager that indicates the number of departures, arrivals, walk-ins, stayovers, and no-shows
- **rooms forecast:** the projection of room sales for a specific period
- **room status:** information on availability of entry to a guest room—reservation (open, confirmed, guaranteed, or repair) or housekeeping (ready, on change, or out-of-order)
- **rule-of-thumb method for determining room rates:** guideline stipulating that the room rate should be $1 for every $1,000 of construction costs (this figure is from the 1960s; the current figure is $2 for every $1,000 of construction costs)
- **safety committee:** a group of frontline employees and supervisors who discuss safety issues concerning guests and employees
- **sales associate:** a person who books the guest's requirements for banquets and other special events
- **sales indicators:** number of guests and revenue generated
- **self-check-in process:** a procedure that requires the guest to insert a credit card having a magnetic stripe containing personal and financial data into a self-check-in terminal and answer a few simple questions concerning the guest stay
- **service management program:** a management program that highlights a company's focus on meeting customers' needs and allows a hotel to achieve its financial goals
- **service strategy statement:** a formal recognition by management that the hotel will strive to deliver the products and services desired by the

guest in a professional manner

- **shift leader:** the person responsible for directing the efforts of a particular work shift
- **single-sheet:** a type of printer that uses single-sheet paper
- **skill demonstration:** demonstration of specific tasks required to complete a job
- **sleeper:** a room that is thought to be occupied but is in fact vacant
- **smart card:** an electronic device with a computer chip that allows a guest or an employee access to a designated area, tracking, and debit-card capabilities for the hotel guest
- **software:** computer-designed applications that process data such as guest information and aid in financial transactions and report generation
- **statement of cash flows:** a projection of income from various income-generating areas of the hotel
- **surcharge rates:** telephone rates for adding service charges for out-of-state long-distance telephone service
- **tax cumulative total feature:** an electronic feature of a PMS that adds all posted room tax amounts previously entered into one grand total
- **telephone initiation and reception agreements:** contracts between senders and receivers of PictureTel concerning specifications of the telephone call and who pays for the call
- **telephone operator:** the person who handles incoming and outgoing calls, locates registered guests and management staff, deals with emergency communication, and assists the desk clerk and cashier when necessary
- **tickler files:** files used to prompt notice that certain events will be occurring
- **top down:** a sales method that involves presenting the most expensive rate first
- **total quality management (TQM:** a management technique that encourages managers to look at processes used to produce products and services with a critical eye
- **total restaurant sales figure:** total of all sales incurred at restaurants or food outlets in the hotel
- **touch screen:** a type of computer monitor screen that allows the operator to input data by touch
- **tractor-fed:** a type of printer that uses a continuous roll of paper

- **traffic managers:** persons who direct hotel guests to available elevators in the lobby
- **training tickler file:** a database that keeps track of training sessions and alerts trainers to important upcoming dates
- **transfer slip:** a form used to transfer an amount of money from one account to another while creating a paper trail
- **travel directories:** organized listings of hotel reservation access methods and hotel geographic and specific accommodations information
- **traveler's checks:** prepaid checks that have been issued by a bank or other financial organization
- **trial balance:** a first run on a set of debits to determine their accuracy against a corresponding set of credits
- **true integration:** the sharing of a reservation database by a hotel's central reservation system and property management system
- **understays:** guests who arrive on time but decide to leave before their predicted date of departure
- **upsell:** to encourage a customer to consider buying a higher-priced product or service than originally anticipated
- **visual alarm systems:** flashing lights that indicate a fire or other emergency in a hotel room
- **walking a guest with a reservation:** offering accommodations at another hotel to a guest who has a reservation when your hotel is overbooked
- **walk-in guests:** guests who request a room rental without having made a reservation
- **working supervisor:** a person who participates in the actual work performed while supervising
- **yield:** the percentage of income that could be secured if 100 percent of available rooms are sold at their full rack rate
- **yield management:** a process of planning to achieve maximum room rates and most profitable guests (guests who will spend money at the hotel's food and beverage outlets, gift shops, etc.), which encourages front office managers, general managers, and marketing and sales directors to target sales periods and develop sales programs that will maximize profit for the hotel
- **yield percentage:** the effectiveness of a hotel at selling its rooms at the highest rate available to the most profitable guest

- **zip drive:** a computer accessory that holds data; a 100-megabyte Zip drive holds an equivalent of 70 floppy disks
- **zip or postal code:** an individual local postal designation assigned by a country.

# CHAPTER THREE

# Career in House Keeping Services

## *Introduction:*

In the traditional literature of India there are many references that hospitality was deeply ingrained in the culture. It was however on an individual or more of not formally organized, later the Buddhist monasteries provided food & lodging for travellers. In the regime of Chandragupta Maurya inns and Atithi Shala's were developed. In Mughul period sarais became popular near Grand Trunk Road. GT Road / Shershah Suri Marg was responsible for great enlargement for the number of lnns/ Sarais in India. In northern India caravanserais were established at the time of Akbar. In the British rule Dak-Bungalows came into being as lodges for government officials.

The modem India has witnessed the growth of star hospitality. The entire business of any hotel involves around only one aspect-"GUEST". The hygiene is essential. A guest spends more time alone in his room than he spends alone in any part of hotel. Thus the attention goes towards cleanliness. The international traveller is more particular towards cleanliness of areas. They get annoyed if the comfort level is not up to their levels. They also get opportunities to compare the quality standards as they visit many places round the world. Housekeeping is the department which is perhaps responsible to bring back a guest to the hotel again and again this is because guests want personal recognition.

House -keeping department has ample scope to pay specials attention to all guest, thus making them feel Important. Housekeeping is open to general inspection. It has no secrets and cannot hide dust and dirt or poor services.

Moreover, this is the department which is indirectly responsible for earning the maximum revenue for the hotel, because the rooms sold by the front office are the rooms made by the House -Keeping. Besides guest rooms, housekeeping has to look after all other areas and is not an easy task to keep the whole hotel sparkling. Thus, justifying the motto —A Hotel is a home away from homel.

As the name suggests housekeeping emphasis on the overall upkeep of house. However, house in our context is hotel. Depending on the size of hotel, the size of this department & workload can easily be accessed. From small to medium or large to huge. In various star hotels, the criterion has not been to satisfy the guest expectations but to exceed its expectations and in order to do so the back bone (Undoubtedly is Housekeeping) should give constant support 24 hrs a Day, 365 days a year. This in itself speaks about the importance of this Department' Maintaining guest rooms, pest control, waste disposal, looking after laundry are some of the major areas, which need, housekeeping concern. However the area is still expanding. Hence, we can say that housekeeping helps in building the image of property in front of the guest.

Housekeeping can rightly be called soul of a hotel if front office is considered to be the heart of a hotel. It is the housekeeping which gets the room ready for the guest and when guest checks out room is handed over to the housekeeping for up-keeping. Items and gadgets to be checked range from bathroom kits to bedroom gadgets like television, refrigerators, and air conditioners and if any fallacy is found with any of the technical equipments, engineering department may be contacted for repairing of the same. Job of the each player of housekeeping department is clearly mentioned in the organization chart so as to avoid duplication of efforts as well as consequent wastage of energy. It is essential that proper inventory shall be maintained so that guests" requirements can be met at all the. In fact, even other segments of the tourism industry ought to know about these services in order to acquaint their clients of the facilities when they sell the packages tours etc.

The housekeeping department has not given its due importance in hotels, particularly in the Indian In this unit you have studied the layout of all types of hotel rooms, linen room, control desk, floor pantry and. A housekeeping professional is a package of behaviours called attributes. Being a service industry, the personal projection of staff to guests enhances the image of hotel. It is also essential to the qualities that a housekeeping staff must possess. These attributes sometimes override the importance of skill, as skill can be taught but these personal traits should be inherent in a member of the staff.

The Housekeeping Department is responsible for cleanliness, maintenance and aesthetic upkeep of the entire hotel. In this unit, we discussed the need for an organisational structure of the housekeeping department, the role of executive housekeeper in organizing the department and the hierarchy of both large and small hotels. We also emphasized on the duties and responsibilities of housekeeping personnel along with the qualities and attributes required for smooth functioning.

The housekeeping is the department of a hotel charged with cleaning and maintaining rooms and public spaces. The housekeeping department is responsible for the daily cleaning of public rooms (lobbies, corridors, meeting rooms), private bedrooms and public washrooms. In addition, it handles the laundering of linens and in some instances, guest laundry as well. For a pleasant stay, guest expects Comfort, Cleanliness and Hygiene, Privacy, Safety and Security and Décor. Housekeeping department holds the responsibility of cleaning, maintenance and efficient upkeep of the hotel. The main functions of housekeeping is Overall cleanliness, bed making, ensures maintenance of the building and its infrastructure, laundry, linen management, key control, pest control, safety and security of the guests as well as the infrastructure and interior decoration. The housekeeping department co-ordinates with other departments to provide high quality services.

## *PERSONAL ATTRIBUTES OF HOUSEKEEPING STAFF*

The housekeeping department in a hotel may easily have the largest work force. No matter how luxurious the decor or how aesthetic the guestroom may be, grumpy, poorly trained , and unhelpful staff can destroy any potential customer satisfaction with the hospitality product. Being a service industry, the personal projection of staff to guests enhances the image of the hotel. It is also essential to know the qualities that a housekeeping staff must possess for the purpose of recruitment, induction, training, and self- development programmes. These attributes sometimes override the importance of skill, as skills can be taught but these personal traits should be inherent in a member of the staff

**Pleasant personality**

A pleasant personality is the result of good grooming and good presentation in front of guests. The way staff looks is the first impression he/ she creates, and this reflects on the quality of service and standards in an establishment. It is good to remember that 'your last look in the mirror will be the guest's first look'. All the supervisory housekeeping staff and the guestroom attendants should be especially well groomed, as they come into close contact with the guests. The staff should be turned out in clean and crisp uniforms. Aftershaves and perfumes used should not be too strong; mild deodorants should be preferred. Most establishments follow a minimum jewellery and light make up policy for female housekeeping staff. Hair must always be clean and, in case of long hair, should be tied up or back. Many hotels have a maid's cap for attendants. Because of the long hours involved, housekeeping staff should wear comfortable, light low-heeled box shoes and keep them looking clean at all times. Unclean mannerisms such as scratching of the face or scalp and chewing gum in front of guests should be avoided. It should always be remembered that a ready smile on face wins many a battle.

**Physical fitness**

Housekeeping is a 24*7*365 operation and the staff work long hours on their feet. Most of their work is manual and may require them to handle heavy equipment. Hence, physical fitness is a must to cope with the nature of this work. A thorough medical examination and a medical history of candidates can be used as tools to ascertain their fitness at the time of recruitment. Housekeeping staff must maintain their level of fitness at the optimum to perform to required standards. It is said that ideal housekeeping staff should possess a 'strong heart and good feet'.

**Personal hygiene**

Personal hygiene deals with matters pertaining to the health of the individual for the maintenance of which the responsibilities lie with him alone. Elements of personal hygiene include:

- Good and healthy habits
- Cleanliness and the skin
- Cleanliness and care of hair, eyes, ears, teeth and nose

- Cleanliness of the nails and fingers
- Cleanliness, tidiness, and condition of clothes and footwear

Housekeeping staff must maintain a high standard of personal hygiene, as it reflects on the hygiene standards of the hotel. They must take a bath daily to avoid body odour. Their hair must be well combed, their nails clean and clipped. Their mouth should be free of any offensive odour. Any infection should be reported and attended to immediately. Cuts and burns should be covered with correct dressings

**Eye for detail**

This is one of the foremost attributes that housekeeping staff must possess. They must be able to take into consideration minute details that a layman may let go unobserved. The power of critical observation is what distinguishes good service from average. Room attendants need to have an eye for detail in order to make up a flawless guestroom and housekeeping supervisors need to have a keen sense of observation to inspect these rooms for perfection. Furthermore, the whole property must be continually scrutinized by the housekeeping department for proper care and maintenance

**Cooperation**

Housekeeping staff must cooperate not only with each other, but also with the staff of other departments. This is absolutely essential, since housekeeping involves a lot of team-work for efficient functioning. If there is any lack of cooperation and coordination, it indirectly affects the guests and hampers efficiency.

**Adaptability**

This is an important quality in housekeeping staff. They should be willing to try out and experiment with new ideas. The entry of foreign hotel chains into India has brought about an immense sense of competition, due to which hotels in India are now trying out more innovative methods and materials in housekeeping. The staff should accept and adapt to change willingly and should welcome such innovations.

**Honesty**

This quality is all-important to the staff in dealings with both guests and the management. Housekeeping staff have direct access to guestrooms. Guests belongings are often left lying around the room and temptations are great. Housekeeping staff also deal with various kinds of guest amenities that may also tempt them. It is inherent discipline and integrity that checks these temptations. If there is trust and respect across the triangle of staff, guests, and management relationships, then there will be a work atmosphere that encourages efficiency and a good team spirit

**Tact and diplomacy**

Housekeeping staff come into close contact with various kinds of guests. Some guest may make unusual requests or complaints. Sometimes guests may be fussy and demand services that override the management's policies. It requires a lot of tact and diplomacy on the part of housekeeping staff to handle such guests at their level, since under no circumstances can they be rude to a guest or hurt his/ her sentiments. Staffs needs to be trained in handling guests who make such requests.

**Right attitude**

Most managers agree that a candidate with the right attitude is more of an asset to them than a candidate who has the skills but the wrong attitude. The candidate with good attitude displays an even temper, courtesy, and good humour, and does not betray displeasure even in most difficult of times. They learn from their mistakes and are always optimistic. The employee with the right attitude is proactive and anticipates the guest's needs and wishes.

**Calm demeanour**

Housekeeping staff may be faced with various kinds of emergency situations, and it is essential that they remain calm so as to o their best in coping with the problem in hand. If they panic during an emergency, their anxious demeanour could become contagious and be passed on to guests and colleagues. A calm demeanour helps employees to think rationally themselves and to display their presence of mind

**Courtesy**

A housekeeping employee should extend courtesy to both guests and colleagues. It is essential that while dealing with the guests, the staff be humble and polite. Housekeeping staff should never argue with a guest and, if they cannot deal with the situation, it should be referred immediately to a senior member of the team. Guests will always remember pleasant and charming staff, as this adds to the guest's experience in a hotel

**Punctuality**

This too is crucially important. If an employee is continually late for duty, it shows lack of interest in the work and a lack of respect for the management and guests. Respect for time during working hours will reflect on the employee's work and help to create an impression worthy of appreciation.

**Good memory**

This is an essential asset in housekeeping staff, particularly when dealing with regular guests and repeat customers. A staff member, who remembers a guest's likes, dislikes, needs, and wishes will be a tremendous asset to the hotel.

**Loyalty**

An employee's first obligation and loyalty are to the establishment in which they are employed and to its management. A situation should never arise when employees use guests as their sounding board. They should respect the policies and decisions of the management.

# ROLE OF HOUSEKEEPING IN GUEST SATISFACTION

Housekeeping may be defined as' provision of a clean, comfortable, safe and aesthetically appealing environment'. By another definition, 'housekeeping is an operational department in a hotel, which is responsible for cleanliness, maintenance, aesthetic upkeep of rooms, public areas, back areas and the surroundings'.

**Comfort:** Achieve the maximum efficiency possible in the care and comfort of the guests and in providing support services for the smooth running of the hotel. Every hotel spends a lot of effort in ensuring the quality of beds, mattresses, channel music, TV, air conditioner if applicable, attached bar etc. The comforts must be regularly maintained and should be properly functioning. It is the duty of the housekeeping department to ensure comfort and a welcoming atmosphere to the guests as well as strive to extend courteous, reliable and satisfactory service from staffs of all departments.

**Cleanliness and Hygiene:** Ensure a high standard of cleanliness and general upkeep in all areas. Clean and well maintained areas and equipments create a favourable impression on the guest. Hygiene is maintained especially in the wash rooms, toilets, pool changing room, health club, etc.

**Privacy:** The prime concern of any guest, irrespective of whether rich or poor, common man or celebrity, is privacy. Room windows are provided with curtains. Windows could normally overlook good scenic view, away from the prying eyes of others in the hotel or outside public. Housekeeping staffs ensure the privacy of the guests and they should be trained with proper procedures to enter the room.

**Safety and Security:** Security is one of the prime concerns of a hotel guest. The housekeeping department staffs should ensure the safety and security of the guests with the help of security services. They should also make sure that fire fighting equipments and emergency alarms are functional at all times. They should also ensure peace, quiet and noise free atmosphere in the area.

**Décor:** Creating a pleasant and classy ambience is also one of the major concerns for a guest. This is not easy and requires a good eye for detail. This work is an art and the housekeeping staffs are mainly responsible for creating a pleasant atmosphere.

## *FUNCTIONS OF HOUSEKEEPING:*

Housekeeping department holds the responsibility of cleaning, maintenance and admirable upkeep of the hotel. The main functions of housekeeping are overall cleanliness, bed making, ensuring maintenance of the building and its infrastructure, laundry, linen management, key control, pest control, safety and security of the guests as well as the infrastructure and interior decoration. All this ensures the ambience and promotes a congenial environment. The basic function of the housekeeping is explained briefly:

**Cleaning Rooms and Public Areas**

Housekeeping department cleans the rooms and toilets and wash basins in the room. Apart from cleaning the guest rooms, housekeeping department is also responsible for cleaning floor, terraces, elevators, elevator lobbies, corridors of guest floors, floor linen closets, mop and janitor's closets, service lobbies and service stairways, function rooms, shopping arcade, cabanas, bars, dining rooms, offices, uniform rooms, tailor rooms, upholstery, shops, store rooms and swimming pools. To be concise, the housekeeping department is responsible for the total cleanliness of a hotel.

**Bed Making**

A guest requires a comfortable bed to take rest, relax and enjoy. A bed that is well- made will provide the required comfort. Bed making is a skill that requires to be developed by the housekeeper, as it not only provides comfort to the guest, but also adds to the pleasant ambience of a guest's room. Guests should not be able to tell if anyone has slept in the room, so a clean environment and perfect bed making is major consideration of this department.

**Linen Management**

One of the important jobs of the Housekeeping Department is clothes and linen management. This involves all functions from purchase of linen to laundering, storage, supplies and to condemnation. In a hotel different types of clothes and linen are used such as the bed sheets, pillow covers, napkins, towels, hand towels, table covers, curtains, cushion covers etc. All of these require regular maintenance.

**Laundry Services**

It is the job of the Housekeeping Department to ensure clean and hygienic washing of all the linen items, and then distributing them to different areas of the hotel. The relationship between the housekeeping and laundry is significant for the smooth functioning of housekeeping services. One of the supporting roles of the laundry is to provide valet services to house guests.

**Pest Control**

Pest Control is another major job of the Housekeeping Department. No matter how clean one keeps the surroundings, one cannot avoid the "uninvited guests" – the pests. It is not only embarrassing but also speaks badly of a hotel where one sees rats, cockroaches, and lizards running around. Therefore, pest control is one of the primary responsibilities of the housekeeping department.

**Key Control**

Key control is one of the major jobs of the housekeeping department. The room keys has to be handled efficiently and safely before and after letting the room.

**Safety and Security**

The Housekeeping Department is responsible for maintaining a peaceful atmosphere in the hotel. If the guests and staff always fear for their safety and the safety of their belongings, the atmosphere will be very tense. Hence the housekeeping department staff should be aware of ways to protect himself and others, especially the guests around him and the property of the hotel from accidents and theft. Several accidents could occur at the place of work. These include fire accidents, falls, wounds,

Injuries, negligence in handling electrical equipment etc . It is important for all housekeeping personnel to know about first aid as they could be the first ones on the spot to give immediate attention to a guest and also an employee in trouble.

## Interior Decoration

Interior decoration is the art of creating a pleasant atmosphere in the living room with the addition of a complex of furnishings, art, and crafts, appropriately combined to achieve a planned result or design. These arts and crafts have to be well maintained by the housekeeping department. Decorating flowers is a creative and stimulating art which often carries a message or theme. Flowers and indoor plants add colour and beauty to a room.

## Room Maintenance

Good housekeeping department is just as responsible for the hotel's maintcnance as an engineering department. In an ideal environment, t h e housekeeping staff and managers should act as the eyes and ears of the engineering department. If damaged or broken items are not reported, they can't be fixed. Proper maintenance will make the perception of cleanliness easier to maintain and reduce guest complaints

# *DUTIES AND RESPOSIBILITIES OF HOUSEKEEPING STAFF*

**Housekeeping staff can be divided into three categories:**
**Managerial** executive housekeeper, head housekeeper
**Supervisory** assistant housekeeper, floor housekeeper, linen room supervisor, public area supervisor and so on
**Unskilled** room attendants, house persons, cloak room attendant
**EXECUTIVE HOUSE KEEPER:**
Reports to: General Manager/ Resident manager / Room division manager

She is responsible and accountable for the total cleanliness and aesthetic upkeep of the hotel. She supervises all housekeeping employees, has the authority to hire or discharge subordinates, plans and assigns work assignments, informs new employees of property regulations, inspects completed assignments, and requisition supplies

**Duties and Responsibilities**

The executive house keeper is expected to

- Organise, supervise, and coordinate the work of housekeeping personnel on a day-to day basis
- Ensure excellence in housekeeping sanitation, safety, comfort, and aesthetics for hotel guests
- Draw up duty rosters and supervise the discipline and conduct of her staff
- Assure proper communication within the department by conducting regular meetings with all personnel
- Hire new employees, warn employees when hotel policies are violated, and discharge employees when necessary
- Counsel employees on various duties and on work- related issues
- Motivate her staff and keep their morale high
- Establish and maintain standard operating procedures for cleaning and to initiate new procedures to increase the efficiency of labour and product use
- Search constantly for and test new techniques and products
- Maintain an inventory of the furniture, linen and movable equipment in the rooms and related premises and to ensure they are regularly checked
- Organize maintenance and repair of guest rooms
- Deal with articles that a guest may have left behind in a room
- Ensure the provision of proper uniforms for the hotel staff
- Ensure observance of hygiene and safety precautions
- Offer suggestions to the human resource department concerning selection, recruitment, replacement, duty alterations, up gradation and so on
- Evaluate employees in order to upgrade them when openings arise
- Organize and supervise on-the-job and off-the-job training of staff
- Liaise between the maintenance and housekeeping departments
- Inspect and approve all supply requisitions for the housekeeping department, and to maintain par stock, inventory control, and cost-

control procedures for all materials
- Check the reports file and the registers maintained
- Maintain a time logbook for all employees within the department
- Be responsible for the redecoration and refurbishing of rooms, lobbies, and so on
- Provide a budget to the management, and undertake budget control and forecasting

## **DEPUTY HOUSE KEEPER:**

Reports to: Executive house keeper

Large hotels may have a deputy house keeper to whom the assistant housekeepers report. In smaller hotels, there may be either an assistant house keeper or a deputy housekeeper reporting to the executive housekeeper

**Duties and Responsibilities**

The deputy housekeeper is expected to

- Check and ensure that all guestrooms, public areas, and ' back-of –the-house' areas are clean and well maintained
- Inspect the work done by contractors, for example, pest control, laundry, window cleaning, and so on.
- Prepare staff schedules and duty rotas
- Ensure periodical stock-taking and maintaining of stock records for linen, uniforms, and equipment
- Provide the necessary information to and assist the executive officer in staff appraisal, disciplining, termination, and promotion
- Develop and implement training programmes within the house keeping department in consultation with the executive house keeper
- Assist the executive house keeper in forecasting and budgeting for operating and capital expenditures
- Take charge of the house keeping department in the absence of the executive house keeper

## **ASSISTANT HOUSE KEEPER/ HOUSEKEEPING MANAGER:**

Reports to: Executive house keeper

The assistant house keeper manages the resources provided by the executive house keeper to achieve the objective of cleanliness, maintenance and attractiveness during a given shift. His/ Her responsibility involves the daily supervision of specific areas within the hotel. In the absence of the deputy house keeper, all the above mentioned duties and responsibilities are taken over by the assistant house keeper

**Duties and Responsibilities**

The assistant house keeper is expected to

- Be responsible for the efficient and orderly management of cleaning, servicing and repairing of guest rooms
- Be responsible for the hotel linen and check its movements and its distribution to room attendants
- Keep an inventory of all housekeeping supplies and check it regularly
- Assist the room attendants in their work
- Provide the front office with a list of rooms ready for allotment to guests
- Organize the flower arrangements
- Arrange the training of staff and substitute for the executive house keeper in case of his/ her absence
- Update record books, registers and files
- Compile the maid's roster
- Check the VIP and OOO rooms

## FLOOR HOUSE KEEPER/ FLOOR SUPERVISOR:

Reports to: assistant house keeper

Floor house keeper has final responsibility for the condition of guestrooms. Each floor house keeper is assigned three or more floors. She gives the room attendants their room assignments and the floor master keys which are returned at the end of the day. She checks, supervises, and approves the attendants work and makes periodical inspection of the physical condition of all rooms on the floor

**Duties and responsibilities**

The floor house keeper is expected to

- Supervise the handing over of soiled linen to the laundry and the requisitioning of fresh ones from house keeping
- Ensure supply of equipment and maintenance and cleaning supplies to floors and public areas
- Issue floor keys to room attendants
- Supervise spring cleaning
- Report on maintenance work on her floor

- Coordinate with room service for cleaning
- Maintain par stock for the respective floors
- Coordinate with the front office manager
- Facilitate the provision of extra services to guests, such as baby sitters, hot water bottles and so on, on request
- Immediately report any safety or security hazard to the security department or to the management
- Check on scanty baggage
- Prepare housekeeping status reports
- Supervise cleaning on the allotted floors and areas- including guest rooms, corridors, stair cases, and floor pantries of the allotted floors
- Report on standards of individual staff performance

## PUBLIC AREA SUPERVISORS:

Reports to: assistant house keeper

Public areas are the 'front-of-the-house' areas such as the entrance, lobby, guest corridors, and so on. Since much of the public area cleaning is done at night, good co ordination with the night supervisor is essential in this role

### Duties and Responsibilities

The public area supervisor is expected to

- Ensure that all public areas and other functional areas are kept clean at all times
- Organize special cleaning of public areas
- Ensure that all maintenance jobs are attended to in co ordination with the maintenance department
- Ensure that flower arrangements are placed in appropriate places in the public areas
- Ensure that banquet halls and conference halls are kept ready for functions and conferences

## NIGHT SUPERVISOR:

Reports to: assistant house keeper

The night supervisor supervises all night staff engaged in the cleaning of public areas and guest rooms in the hotel

### Duties and Responsibilities

The night supervisor is expected to

- Ensure that all public areas are thoroughly cleaned at night, which is the only time when traffic is low
- Clear departure rooms to the front office if necessary
- Plan the order of work according to priority and direct the staff accordingly
- Make sure that departure rooms are serviced and made ready as soon as possible in order that reception may re- let at any time
- Organize special cleaning of rooms as required
- Anticipate guest's requirements at all times, thereby ensuring comfort and satisfaction
- See that all lost-and-found articles are deposited with the control desk
- Ensure the submission of room attendant's reports and the room status report
- Help with the training of staff
- Report any safety and security hazard

### EVENING SHIFT SUPERVISOR:

Reports to: assistant house keeper

Evening shift supervisors are required for the floors, public areas, and control room.

**Duties and Responsibilities**

- An evening shift supervisor is expected to
- Check all log entries and ensure they are followed up
- Ensure all keys are deposited back before taking over the shift
- Ensure the cleaning of rooms that were not serviced in the morning – rooms with a 'do not disturb', double locked, or refused service status
- Ensure all departure rooms are cleaned and released to the front office as soon as possible
- Ensure that the turndown service is carried out for all rooms
- Ensure public areas are kept clean at all times

### LINEN ROOM SUPERVISOR/ LINEN KEEPER:

Reports to: assistant house keeper

The linen supervisor supervises the work of the linen room and may have several linen attendants to assist her in providing clean, presentable linen throughout the house

**Duties and responsibilities**

The linen room supervisor is expected to

- Be responsible for the entire hotel's linen
- Send dirty linen to the laundry after checking them piece by piece
- Check laundered linen before giving it for ironing
- Put away linen neatly once it has been washed, ironed, and mended
- Hand out linen to the various departments on presentation of vouchers signed by the heads of the respective departments
- Maintain a register of linen movements and check the linen regularly
- Look after the ironing and laundering of guests clothes and the uniforms of the hotel staff
- Supervise the work of the linen attendants and tailors
- Make suggestions relating to replacement purchases

## UNIFORM ROOM SUPERVISOR:

Reports to: assistant house keeper

The uniform room supervisor is responsible for the maintenance of hotel staff uniforms

**Duties and Responsibilities**

- The uniform room supervisor is expected to
- Be responsible for providing clean, serviceable uniforms to the staff of the host
- Keep an inventory control of various uniforms in various stages of use- such as when sorted ones are handed over, or which are being washed or dry- cleaned in the laundry, or those on the person of the staff, or those in store for future issue
- Set the budget for the procurement of additional material for staff uniforms

## LINEN ROOM ATTENDANT/ LINEN ROOM MAID:

Reports to: linen room supervisor

**Duties and responsibilities**

The linen room attendant is expected to

- Be responsible for sorting all the sheets, pillow cases, towels, table cloths, napkins, and so on to separate stacks
- Issue clean linen on a clean-for-soiled basis

- Place soiled linen in containers and send those to the laundry
- Examine and count each item when they are sent to the laundry and again on their return
- Shelve laundered linen after verifying the number and type of articles
- Send torn articles to the seamstress for repair
- Maintain proper records of discards and determine the percentage of discards

## UNIFORM ROOM ATTENDANT:

Reports to: uniform room supervisor

The uniform room attendant is in actual contact with the staff for the issue of uniforms

**Duties and responsibilities**

A uniform room attendant is expected to

- Issue clean uniforms while received soiled ones
- Send soiled uniforms for laundering
- Examine the laundered items to ensure cleanliness and serviceability
- Send torn uniforms to the seamstress for mending
- Keep a count of uniforms
- Shelve laundered uniforms after verifying the types of articles
- Count and record linen to fill requisitions

## STORE KEEPER:

Reports to: linen room supervisor

**Duties and Responsibilities**

A store keeper is expected to

- Control the stock of equipment
- Store cleaning materials and agents
- Issue equipment and cleaning materials as per demand
- Prepare requisitions for used-up materials and new products for the approval of the executive house keeper
- Liaise with the purchase department for the procurement of approved materials

## CONTROL DESK SUPERVISOR/ CONTROL ROOM SUPERVISOR:

Reports to: assistant house keeper

The control room or control desk is the nerve centre of the house keeping department. The desk is manned 24 hours a day. Since the control desk is the hub of information dissemination in housekeeping, the control desk supervisor is a critical person in housekeeping operations.

**Duties and Responsibilities**

The control desk supervisor is expected to

- Coordinate with the front office for information on departure rooms and handing over of clean rooms
- Coordinate with other departments for smooth functioning and efficiency
- Receive complaints on maintenance and house keeping
- Maintain registers kept at the control desk
- Receive special requests from guests
- Act as a pivotal person in receiving and disseminating information amongst house keeping staff
- Maintain the latest reports regarding room occupancy, VIPs , status of rooms, and so on, so that work can be delegated to attendants and supervisors accordingly
- Attend to all phone calls received at the control desk
- Be responsible for guest room keys given to room attendants and to store the keys and maintain a key register

**<u>GUEST ROOM ATTENDANTS/ ROOM MAIDS/CHAMBER MAIDS:</u>**

Reports to: floor supervisor

Guest room attendants work is of great importance because it contributes in a big way to the comfort of guests and hence, their impression of the hotel and this includes making beds, coping with linen supplies, and general cleaning. Nowadays, most hotels use the term 'attendant' rather than 'maid' since men have entered this arena earlier dominated by women

**Duties and Responsibilities**

A room attendant is expected to

- Clean and tidy rooms as per the sanitary regulations assigned
- Change guestroom and bathroom linen
- Make guest room beds
- Replenish guest supplies

- Answer guests summons promptly
- Be responsible for getting guest laundry processed
- Undertake the evening check of rooms and provide the turn- down service
- Check and secure rooms
- Hand over to the house keeper any article which a guest might have left behind in a room
- Replenish the maid's cart with guest supplies, cleaning agents, and linen

## HEAD HOUSE PERSON:

Reports to: public area supervisor

**Duties and Responsibilities**

The head house person is expected to

- Supervise the work allotted to house persons, especially those in the public areas
- Supervise the work of people who clean the carpets, wall washers, and window washers
- Supervise the work of drapery men, heavy vacuum machine operators for general cleaning, chandelier cleaners, and workers responsible for re-lamping
- Supervise the work of furniture men, floor men, and warehouse men

## HOUSE PORTERS/ HOUSE PERSONS:

Reports to: head house person/ public area supervisor

The house person's job involves heavy physical work as assigned, such as carpet cleaning, window cleaning, carrying heavy pieces of furniture, washing public areas, garbage clearance, and also complementing the work of room attendants on guest floors

**Duties and Responsibilities**

A house person is expected to

- Clean carpets
- Shift beds, chairs, and other heavy furniture
- Cart linen to and from floors
- Clean the swimming pool
- Clean garden paths and such outdoor surfaces
- Clean out the garbage

- Polish all brassware
- Help room attendants in their work in guest rooms
- Clean all doors, windows, and ventilators
- Take down and re- hang curtains as needed
- Clean fire – fighting equipment
- Keep the fire buckets filled with sand
- Take on heavy cleaning of areas such as shafts and terraces
- Wash walls, draperies, chandeliers, and other hard-to reach-areas

## <u>TAILORS, SEAMSTRESSES AND UPHOLSTERERS:</u>

Reports to: linen room supervisor

They are responsible for mending and stitching uniforms, linen, and upholstery, respectively. The upholsterers also replenish upholstery that require replacement

**Duties and Responsibilities**

This group of staff are expected to

- Mend all damaged linen using methods such as patching
- Mend all damaged uniforms and alter uniforms if required
- Make pads from used mattress pads for the burnishing of silver
- Stitch pillowcases if required
- Refurnish all damaged upholstery
- Repair guests clothes if damaged
- Estimate the requirement of materials and request the linen room supervisor to place a requisition at the stores
- Draw material from the stores and take these to the tailoring room
- Pre- shrink material whenever required

## <u>CLOAK ROOM ATTENDANT/ POWDER ROOM ATTENDANT:</u>

Reports to: public area supervisor

**Duties and Responsibilities**

The cloak room attendant is expected to

- Maintain an adequate stock of soaps, detergents, combs, brushes, powder, and hand towels to meet demands at peak hours
- Take soiled hand towels to the linen room for replacement
- Maintain the shoe-shine kit and clean guest's shoes if required
- Maintain all cupboards and fixtures installed in the cloakroom

- Brush guests jackets if required

## HAT CHECKER:

A hat checker provides his services in superior hotels in cold climates. His domain is the hat check room, where hats and heavy overcoats are deposited by guests as soon as they enter the hotel lobby, so as to spare them the inconvenience of carrying these articles around in the hotel. The hat checker carefully labels these guest articles, and hangs or stores them correctly so as to return them to the guests when they are leaving the hotel

## HORTICULTURIST:

Reports to: assistant house keeper

He/ she leads a team of gardeners in maintaining the landscaped gardens of the hotel as well as in supplying flowers from the gardens for flower arrangements in the hotel. Flowers are used largely by the house keeping departments to aesthetically enhance various areas of the hotel. Flower arrangements may be used in banquet functions, guest rooms, restaurants, lobbies, offices and so on.

**Duties and Responsibilities**

The horticulturist is expected to

- Supervise the maintenance of gardens and landscaped areas
- Ensure a smooth supply of flowers to the house keeping garden
- Assist the executive house keeper with flower arrangements in the absence of a florist

## HEAD GARDENER:

Reports to: horticulturist

He is required to maintain landscaped areas and gardens in a hotel, keeping in mind their cleanliness, aesthetic appeal, and freshness all the year round through a well- motivated team of gardeners

**Duties and Responsibilities**

The head gardener is expected to

- Ensure that landscaped areas, gardens, rock gardens, water ways, and so on, are maintained as per the original concept
- Brief, schedule, and allot duties to gardeners
- Take care of fresh seasonal plantings
- Procure, control, and supervise the usage of manure and fertilizers

- Maintain the watering schedules and attend to any problem regarding water shortages
- Provide the hotel with flowers, garlands, wreaths or bouquets as and when required
- Maintain and prepare indoor plants for the hotel
- Supervise the maintenance of lawns, mowing and replanting the grass
- Train gardeners
- Ensure that gardeners handle equipment and tools effectively and correctly
- Oversee the upkeep of the plant nursery and green house

## <u>GARDENERS:</u>

Gardeners report to the head gardener or the horticulturist. They keep landscaped areas, lawns, and gardens clean, aesthetically beautiful, and fresh through the daily schedules of tasks assigned to them

**Duties and responsibilities**

The gardener is expected to

- Dig landscaped areas and maintain them as per the original concept and undertake fresh plantings
- Plant seeds and saplings as per conditions and the landscaping/ horticultural concept
- Distribute manure and fertilizer appropriately
- Water all garden areas as scheduled
- Maintain the plant nursery and the green house
- Prune and trim hedges and bushes
- Prepare flowers, potted indoor plants, wreaths, bouquets, and so on, as required by the hotel
- Utilize garden tools efficiently

## <u>FLORIST:</u>

Reports to: horticulturist

**Duties and responsibilities**

A florist is expected to

- Collect fresh flowers from the gardener's everyday
- In case flowers are not available from the hotel gardens, to purchase flowers from dealers

- Make up various types of flower arrangements for different hotel areas- lobbies, front office, restaurants, banquet halls, convention rooms, VIP rooms, and guest rooms
- Provide garlands, wreaths, and bouquets to the hotel for guests, as and when required
- Treat cut flowers so that they last longer
- Maintain flower arrangements – by changing water, pruning, and so on
- Be responsible for the functioning of the flower room in the house keeping department, which deals with the care of flower arranging equipment, mechanics, and accessories
- Train the assistant florist

## LAUNDRY MANAGER:

Reports to: executive house keeper

He/ she are responsible for the entire functioning of the laundry and dry- cleaning unit. A laundry manager must have organisational ability as well as technical knowledge of chemicals and their effect on fabrics

## LAUNDRY SUPERVISOR:

He/ she are in charge of the functioning of the laundry in the absence of the laundry manager. A laundry supervisor must have a good understanding of all aspects of the laundry equipment, chemicals and fabrics

## DRY- CLEANER:

The dry-cleaner is in charge of the dry – cleaning of hotel linen and guest clothing

## WASHER:

A washer is the person who actually does the laundering of linen, uniforms, and guest clothing

**Duties and responsibilities**

The washer is expected to

- Spot stained fabrics before loading them into the washing machines
- Load soiled linen into washing machines, feed in the right amount of detergent and other laundering chemicals, and run the machines
- Load washed linen into dryers
- Clean all equipment after use

## LAUNDRY WORKERS:

They are the lower rung of staff in the laundry, carrying out a variety of duties. Proper training is essential to ensure they function smoothly and efficiently

**Duties and responsibilities**

A laundry worker is expected to

- Sort soiled linen according to fabric types, colours, and degree of soiling
- Load soiled linen into washing machines and to load washed linen into dryers
- Transport soiled linen from the linen room to the laundry and fresh linen from the laundry to the linen room
- Keep the laundry clean

<u>**PRESS MEN:**</u>

Press men are responsible for ironing linen, uniforms, and guest clothing using hand irons, calendaring machines, steam presses, and so on

<u>**VALETS/ RUNNERS:**</u>

'Valet service' means that the hotel will take care of the guest's laundry. Valets report to the linen room supervisor. They are responsible for collecting soiled guest laundry and delivering fresh guest laundry. In many hotels, a valet is not charged with the task of delivering guest laundry only. Here the valet shares a service room with the GRAs; the room is complete with iron and ironing board, needles, cotton and string, shoe cleaning necessities, and so on. He may also perform the less tedious functions of a houseman.

## *Situation Handling*

<u>*Keys Theft:*</u>

The locks in hotels are generally spring-operated mortise locks but to overcome the problem of key thefts, keyless lock systems have been devised. They are expensive but are in use in some hotels. They may be computerized but there is also a less expensive battery powered lock system, with an infrared device, which reads the guests, cares.

A disposable plastic card about the size of a conventional credit card replaces the normal metal room key. One of these cards is given to each guest on checking in. In the computerized system the card is coded by perforations at random from a pool of more than four billion potential codes available from a master computer console at the front desk. The random code is then transmitted electronically to the specific guest's room lock and only this particular card can open that room door. When the guest checks out, the code on that room is changed and a new guest will receive a new code on his new check-in card; the old card automatically becomes useless.

Similar cards may be coded as master keys for the maids and housekeepers and can be changed at frequent intervals at reception' Re-keying lock systems may also help to overcome the problem of key theft and a new system allows the lock to be changed quickly and easily without having to take the tumbler apart, without removing the lock from the door and without entering the room. Using a special key, which instantly changes the tumbler, changes the lock.

### *Lost Property:*

It is generally practice that any lost property found in rooms should be handed in to the housekeeper's office immediately (or other place according to house system), and the appropriate details should be entered in a lost properly book, after which the articles should be labeled and will usually be kept for a period of six months. Great tact should be exercised in dealing with lost property and it is advocated that guests are not notified of articles found in rooms unless they are still in the building. Precautions need to be taken to ensure that articles are only handed over to the rightful owner and not to any would be claimant.

### *Valuables:*

Hotels have a safe or safe deposit boxes and notices are displayed asking guests not to leave valuables in their rooms but to have them locked away in the safe. Should a maid come into an occupied room and find valuables left there, she should inform the housekeeper who will deal with them according to house custom. It is less likely that guests will leave valuables about when personal safes are provided in their rooms. Peepholes, which allow guests to see who is outside their door, are considered standard security equipment in some hotels.

### *Other Security Measures:*

The housekeeper is responsible for the reporting of faulty window catches and at night should ensure that all fresh windows and balcony doors are securely locked and that panic bars on fire exit doors are adjusted to enable no entry from outside. tn hotels baby sitters may be arranged by the housekeeper and may be members of the staff or from an agency and both should have a written permit from the housekeeper authorizing them to be on the floors; those from an agency will normally collect the permit from the hall porter as they come into the hotel. Inventories, stock lists etc. kept by the housekeeper should help in discovering the loss of items, e.g. linen, cleaning equipment, etc. through pilfering and as a result investigations should take place.

For security reasons the housekeeper selects her staff carefully and prospective new member of staff should be asked for the names and addresses of one or two persons to whom reference can be made, and testimonials should not be relied on. In taking up references, it is wise, if possible, to talk on the telephone rather than to expect former employers to commit them on paper.

### *Health and Safety Fire and Personal Injury:*

These are hazards in any establishment and their prevention is of tremendous importance. While the management is ultimately responsible for the prevention of accidents, the housekeeper, along with other department heads, should endeavor to see that her staff is safety conscious. Accidents are costly; there may be serious effects on the injured person; time and materials may be lost; a new employee may need to be trained.

Employers have to be responsible if defective equipment, due to its design or manufacture, causes an accident; this may result in compulsory insurance and legal costs. There are a great variety of accidents causing person injury, which may befall guests and staff and while they are normally caused through someone's carelessness they are less likely to occur in a clean, uncluttered and well maintained department'

### *First Aid:*

Illness, accidents and other emergencies to guests and staff unfortunately occur from time to time in any establishment, and while the housekeeper may or may not be the official first aider she may become involved. The employer must provide sufficient first-aid equipment, and facilitate personnel. First aid personnel should be available at all times and staff should know who they are. While a housekeeper should have knowledge of first aid it is essential that she be level headed and able to take command of a situation so that it does not become out of hand and to prevent panic, gossip or consternation spreading throughout the house.

In order to stop the spread of disquieting facts or gossip, staff should be asked to cooperate and be discreet with the guests regarding unfortunate incidents. Inevitably there will be the maid who is anxious to tell the guests of an accident or death which occurred in a certain room and, while it may not worry some guests it will others, and in either case it would be better left unsaid.

In the case of illness a doctor is normally on call and the housekeeper will contact him when necessary, and after the visit she will ensure that his instructions are carried out, in the case of an emergency, an ambulance maybe called. In large establishments, there may be a resident doctor or qualified nurse in attendance (and always a first aider), and this relieves the housekeeper of much responsibility.

In the case of a death being reported to the housekeeper, she tells the manager and a doctor is called immediately. The central heating or air conditioning should be turned off and, to prevent unauthorized persons entering the room, the door is locked until the body is removed.

The removal of the body should be done as unobtrusively as possible, and often takes place at night, or some other quiet time when there are few guests about. In the case of a suspected suicide, any drinking glass, tablets or vomit must be left for the doctor and/or police' as they may be needed as evidence.

## *HOUSEKEEPING TERMINOLOGY*

- Amenities: Services or items offered to guests or placed in the guestrooms for convenience and comfort at no extra cost.
- Antiseptic: An agent that makes the environment non-conducive to the growth and reproduction of disease-causing microbes.
- Back of the house: The functional areas of the hotel in which employees have little or no guest contact, such as the engineering and maintenance department, laundry, and so on.
- Buffing: Polishing, the floor with a low-speed polishing machine.
- Builders: A builder is defined as a compound that has no surface-active properties but increases the bulk and the efficiency of a detergent.
- Burnishing: Polishing the floor with a high-speed floor machine to achieve an extremely high gloss.
- Carborundum: Silicon Carbide, used as an abrasive.

- Caustic Alkalis: Very strong alkalis such as Sodium hydroxide (caustic soda)
- Chamois Leather: Chamois leather is used mainly in cleaning and polishing. Originally skins of chamois goat antelope were used, but now they are usually skivers, that is, split skins of sheep or simulated leather. Chamois leather is used wet for cleaning windows
- Crib: A cot for babies, provided to guest on request.
- Crinkle Sheet: A distinctively woven sheet used to cover and protect the blanket. It is now called a third sheet.
- Damp-dust: A method of cleaning where the item to be cleaned is wiped with a damp cloth.
- Deep Cleaning: Intensive or specialized cleaning undertaken in guestrooms or public areas, often conducted according to a special schedule or on a special project basis.
- Departure Room: A room from which the guest has departed, settled the account, returned the room keys, and left the hotel. It is also called a check out room or vacated room.
- DND Card: A 'do not disturb' card is hung outside the room to inform hotel staff or visitors that the occupant does not wish to be disturbed.
- Dutch Wife: Another term for the sewing kit provided as a guest amenity.
- Duvets: Quilts filled with down feathers or synthetic fibers. Also referred sometimes as comforters.
- Faucets: Another term for taps.
- Floor Pantry: A service room provided on each floor for GRA's to store cleaning agents, equipment, guest supplies, guestroom linen, and maid's cart
- Graveyard Shift: Night Shift
- Guest Loan Items: Guest supplies not normally found in a guestroom, but available upon request-for example, hair dryers and ironing boards.
- H.W.C.: Handle with care
- Hand Caddy: A portable container for storing and transporting cleaning supplies, carried on a room attendant's cart.
- Housekeeping: Housekeeping is defined as the provision of a clean, comfortable, safe, and aesthetically appealing environment
- Inventory: Stocks of merchandise, operating supplies, and other items held for future use in a hospitality operation.
- Kaolin: China Clay

- Lacquer: Colored varnish made of shellac dissolved in alcohol.
- Linen Chute: A passage in the form of a tunnel for sending soiled linen from the floor pantries of all floors to a central place near the laundry, from where it can be collected by the laundry staff
- Linen: Material woven from fibers of the flax plant. The term 'linen' is also used loosely to denote daily launderable articles in the linen room
- Occupancy: The number of rooms actually in use/occupied.
- Ottoman: Sofa without a back.
- pH Scale: A scale that indicates the acidity or alkalinity of substances.
- Quats: Quaternary ammonium compounds, used as disinfectant.
- Sani-bins: Small metal or plastic containers with lids, kept in toilets for the collection of soiled sanitary towels.
- Scanty baggage: A room status indicating a room that is occupied by a guest with small, light luggage.
- SOP: Standard operating procedure. A document of a standing nature that specifies a certain method of operating or a specific procedure for the accomplishment of a task.
- SPATT: Special Attention
- Squeegee: A manual cleaning equipment with a rubber or metal blade and a long handle, used for removing excess moisture from hard surfaces such as floors and window panes.
- Surfactants: Surface-active compounds that impart a good wetting power, emulsifying power, and suspending power to detergents.
- Tarnish: A discouloration caused by a chemical reaction between a metal and substances found in water, air and food. Different metals undergo different types of tarnishing.
- Terrazo: Flooring which consists of marble, granite, and other decorative chips set in cement.
- Tooth-glass /Gargling glass: A glass placed on the vanity unit as a guest supply and used for gargling.
- Upholstery: Textiles, padding, springs and other materials used for decorating furniture and rendering it more comfortable.
- Vanity Unit: A unit comprising a wash basin and mirror, surrounded by a flat area where soap, dental kits, shaving kits, and tooth glasses are kept.
- Veneer: A thin coating of finer wood on another wooden surface
- Water Closet: Sanitary fitting consisting of the toilet bowl and the cistern.
- WC: Water Closet; a toilet bowl and flush.

- Wicker: Wicker is derived from the shoots of willow plants. It is used for making woven items such as bread baskets, flower baskets, mats etc.

## <u>ROOM STATUS CODES: -</u>

- or OCC : Occupied
- Comp. : Complimentary
- DND : Do not disturb
- SB : Scanty Baggage
- V/C : Vacant & Cleaned
- CR : Checked & ready
- OOO : Out Of Order
- DNCO : Did not check out
- CO or C/O : Check-out/vacated/departure room.
- UR : Under-repair room
- NL or NB : No luggage/no baggage
- DL : Double-lock Room

# CHAPTER FOUR

# The Most Important Chapter

## *Preparation for a Job Interview*

Through all the different questions, the interviewing officer is silently trying to gauge your personality, how you work and your ability to deal with stress. It will be impossible for someone to tell you exactly what they are looking for, but there are certain aspects you could work on. Most importantly, you need to have a sense of intuition such that you can read between the lines as the interviewing officer posts questions for you and be intelligent in answering them. A judgment call needs to be made every time in order to do well in the process. Most of the aspirant attend the interview without preparing for the PI, you can answer most of the PI questions if you are good speaker and have clarity of thoughts, but most of the aspirants are not able to perform well during personal interview even though they know what kind of questions they are going to face and what importance these questions hold in the complete interview assessment. Below I have picked some important areas from which you could face most of the questions.

### Family background

One of the most common and primary questions asked during the interview is the family background of the aspirant. Right from the time a child is interviewed for admission to schools to his or her job interviews, this question continues to be an important one. Why is this so? This is because while we are growing up, the family has the maximum influence on us. According to studies, from birth till the age of seven, a child is influenced by the mother's emotions. For the next seven years, it works on the actions taken up by the father. Thereafter, the personality of the child develops which is again the result of the family and the environment of upbringing. The family background thus speaks volumes about the kind of personality one has.

### Mother or the Father?

It is a common theory that girls tend to take the action side of the father while a boy is more inclined to the emotional aspects of the mother. Thus, this tendency to be more like one of the parents than the other could have an impact on the personality you carry. Whether you are emotional in nature or whether you prefer to show your worth with actions is one of the conclusions drawn from it. So, this could be an important question in an interview for observing your behavioural skills.

### Independence

Are you independent in your actions? Can you take decisions independently at work? Or do you always need to rely on someone else's judgments in order to perform well? This is one question that the interviewing officer has in mind and expresses it by asking about your daily routines and schedules are like. Independence is an important trait to have and can prove useful for your professional life. During our childhood, we are extremely and completely dependent on our parents of the family for support. This is gradually withdrawn from our lives as we grow up. This removal of support happens at different stages, in different phases. So when the officer repeatedly asks you about your daily life, the kind of work you do and the schedules you follow, this is the question he wants to be answered. Your routines can also speak volumes about your punctuality, how organized you are in your work. So, make sure you answer these questions with care.

### Social Circle

The social circle is an underrated part of the interview questions. Often it happens that people don't pay much attention to it and tend to answer it casually. But it has a bigger influence on your life than what you would imagine. The kind of friends you have, the intensity of friendships, how much time you spend with them, how long your friendships last are important points to focus on during the interview. It reflects upon the kind of person you are and how well you can adjust in a social group. Another important query can be what are the things that you look for in a friend before establishing companionship?

### Deference

Deference is an important trait to have. This is again something that we learn from our family ambiance or schooling days. If you know how to respect elders and thus cooperate with them, you are in general holding a good personality. Having a sympathetic attitude for everyone, showing empathy to people in need, being generous are some of the qualities that the interviewer is looking forward to in you. The interviewing officer might ask you different questions in order to draw a conclusion about how well you respect others, both peers, and seniors and your ability to work in coordination with others.

### <u>Who do you look up to?</u>

Who do you look up to in life? Who is your role model? Who do you want to emulate in your actions in daily life? This is yet another question drawing light on your personality. Having a role model means you admire someone enough to follow them and carve your life around the same virtues, qualities or discipline. Once you have a real-life hero like that, consciously or unconsciously, you are following his or her footsteps. Whether you know it or not, whether you accept it or not, this real-life hero is in your life in different ways. This has two major implications. One is, you will be following a certain type or quality or traits and secondly, you prefer these kinds of qualities over the others. This gives us a lot of information about the kind of personality one has.

### <u>Team activities</u>

How often do you take part in team activities in your life outside of work? Do you feel competitive in such cases? Are you able to coordinate with the members of your team? These questions can go a long way in determining your team spirit. Often, participation in group tasks speaks volumes about how well you can adapt to changes in the team, strategies and the likes. Also, how well you react to a win or a loss also determines your personality.

### <u>Dealing with failures</u>

Taking the previous concept forward, acceptance of failure is often an important virtue. What happens when you encounter a failure? The first step would be accepting it, getting on with it. Next, you analyze where the work went wrong, regroup with your teammates and ensure that this is not repeated in the future. This is the sequence followed when failure cannot be avoided. The interviewer would want to know how well you are able to abide by this order and whether you can accept blame for your mistakes or not.

### <u>Leadership and responsibilities</u>

Next up is an important test of your personality. You have to be very careful while answering questions about leadership. Every company or organization would want to hire a leader, whether the leadership skills are to be used immediately or later in the career. Taking responsibility willingly, managing a team assigned to you, being able to give instructions and follow them when required are some of the values a good leader must have.

### Hunger for knowledge

It is one thing to have a very qualified person recruited for a particular job. It is a whole other advantage to have a person who wants to keep learning all the time. Every individual should have a certain level of curiosity and the zeal to keep learning. This indicates that you are able to use your current knowledge to do your work, but also keep adapting in order to expand your knowledge base to improve the quality of work delivered.

### Persistent

What would be a better choice for recruitment: A person who tries and gives up on being unsuccessful or a person who is persistent and won't give up till the goal is achieved? The answer is pretty simple. The second kind is the one people want in their teams. It takes a lot of courage, determination, and conviction to keep doing the same thing till the milestone is achieved. Thus, when the interviewer asks you similar questions, ensure that you clearly voice your ideas of being a persistent worker who is ready to work hard in situations of fatigue.

### Why do you want to be here?

This is again one of the most popular questions in any interview. Why do you want to work in that particular organization? Most people make the huge mistake of preparing a strategic answer for this question, usually borrowed from someone, in order to impress the interviewer. But, the person sitting opposite to you knows how to read your eyes and your body language. This answer has to be genuine, expressing a clear and honest interest of working there. This could be the deciding question for your selection, so think twice before answering it. While these are some of the guidelines followed for answering the questions shot at you during the interview, there is a bigger trait that is most desirable. One can stress enough on the importance of intuition during an interview. Being able to think independently, take decisions on the spot are important qualities to have. More importantly, how you work spontaneously, having a presence of mind will help you through this selection process and later likewise in your work life. Above all, it is essential to maintain a calm and cool head to have a positive impression on the interviewer.

# *Communication with Guest and Body language*

## <u>Effective Speaking:</u>

Some speakers are better than the other in getting across their messages, while the others are not that convincing in their oral communication. But according to experts we all can acquire the qualities of a good public speaker with learning and practice.

But before that we have to know what essential qualities churn out an outstanding public speaker.

- **Clear**
- **Relevant**
- **Insightful**
- **Succinct (To the point)**
- **Practiced**
- **Energetic**
- **Respectful**

**Clear** – If you're even slightly vague in your own mind about your core message, or you don't deliver your message in a logical order, with clear transitions from one point to the next – your audience will be confused. It does take time to work all this through, but it's really important. Content is usually the reason why you and your audience are in the same room and thinking it through well enough beforehand makes all the difference to your reception as a speaker.

**Relevant** – You need to know your audience, in as much detail as possible. Audiences are sophisticated, and don't appreciate generalities. Tailor what you're going to say by doing as much research you need to beforehand.

You cannot motivate, inspire, inform, or expect your listeners to 'buy in' to your ideas:

A. Unless you talk their language.

B. If you don't speak at their level of understanding on the subject.

C. If you use jargon and words unfamiliar to them.

**Insightful** – dictionary.reference.com defines the word 'insightful' as — the ability to perceive clearly or deeply; penetration. And Scott Berkun in his great book Confessions of a Public Speaker (O'Reilly 2010) goes so far as to say this: ―The problem with most bad presentations I see is not the speaking, the slides, the visuals, or any of the things people obsess about. Instead, it's the lack of thinking.

**Succinct** – When you're listening to a speaker, no matter how interesting, isn't it true that when they say the magic words ―to sum up‖ or ―finally‖, you wake up? It just seems to be human nature, and one of the best ways to respect your audience is to be as brief as possible!

**Practice** – This is absolutely crucial. And it must be done out loud, at least part of the time. Yes, this is tedious, and most people don't do it, which is why it's a characteristic of good speakers.

**Energy** - Your audience follows your cue: every group who doesn't know you will be cool to start with, we're all metaphorically taking a step back and assessing, in the early moments of hearing a new speaker. But if you show some energy, some life-force, the audience will follow you. You need to set the tone. You can also gain energy from your audience (a topic for another day!).

**Respect** – Every member of your audience wants to feel respected by you as the speaker. And this applies even more as a speaker if an audience member is rude or difficult. No matter how much you want to retaliate, remember that an audience will feel ―as one‖ to some extent, and if you get tetchy with one person, they will potentially all be offended. So even if someone hits your hottest button, continue to be pleasant. That way, you'll gain the respect of the group, and potentially avoid crashing in flames, too!

<u>**Listening and note taking skills:**</u>

Good note taking involves effective listening that includes concentrating on, selecting, summarizing, and finally, evaluating what is being said by the lecturer. The key to effective listening is to be an ACTIVE listener.

<u>**Suggestions to improve your listening skills:**</u>

1. Be prepared. Survey relevant test materials and notes. The more you know, the more interested you will be. Participate in an exchange of ideas rather than a bombardment of unfamiliar ideas and unrelated facts.

2. Acquaint yourself with a lecturer's general lecture method and mannerisms. Pay attention to style, tone inflection of voice, pauses, accentuation of words, and nonverbal cues. Use these as signals for

identifying important points.

3. Try not to be affected or distracted by lecturer's mannerisms.

### Note taking:

Effective note taking involves extracting and recording the important ideas covered in lecture in a way that will help you to recall them. Good notes provide a valuable means for review and learning, and can increase the probability of doing well on an exam.

### Suggestions to Improve your Note taking:

1. Think before writing. Relate what is being said to what you already know or have reviewed. Use your own interests/needs as well as information common to the course to guide your thoughts.

2. Preparing for class is an aid in helping you to become aware of the major concepts and in deciding what to record.

3. Be selective. Listen to everything, but do not try to write it all down. Search for the main ideas and sort out the important sub points and details. Notes should be brief, legible and consistent.

4. Take accurate notes. Use our own words, but don't waste time thinking of synonyms. Lecturer's terms may be simplified later. Use brackets to separate your own ideas from those of the lecturer.

5. Abbreviate words whenever possible, but be consistent.

6. Don't worry about missing a point. Leave spaces and fill what you missed later. Also, leave spaces for expanding and clarifying notes.

7. Record all important facts: dates, names, places, formulas. Copy diagrams and illustrations which will clarify your notes.

8. Draw a single line through mistakes, rather than erase or black out completely. This saves time and energy, and you may find later that the mistakes may have been important to record after all.

9. Integrate lecture notes with text material. This is helpful for clarification and retention of material. If text material is repeated in the lecture, you can make a notation for later referral to the text. Be sure to note supplementary examples or elaborations.

10. Review notes after class. Reread and edit your notes as soon as possible while the information is still fresh in your mind, adding and clarifying in order to increase your understanding. Write a summary (a paragraph or two) or formulate a summary question at the end of your notes to consolidate ideas and to reflect the relationship of facts and ideas with each other and as a whole.

### Body language:

Body language is a form of non-verbal communication. Body language is about using behaviour to communicate. Both people and animals use this form of communication. Part of this behaviour is done subconsciously. It is therefore different from communicating using sign language, for example. Communication using sign language is intentional, body language is not. The forms of behaviour used in body language include body posture, gestures, facial expressions, and eye movements.

Body language may provide clues as to the attitude or state of mind of a person. For example, it may indicate aggression, attentiveness, boredom, a relaxed state, pleasure, amusement and intoxication. Language is significant to communication and relationships. It is relevant to management and leadership in business and also in places where it can be observed by many people. It can also be relevant to some outside of the workplace. It is commonly helpful in dating, mating, in family settings, and parenting.

Although body language is non-verbal or non-spoken, it can reveal much about your feelings and meaning to others and how others reveal their feelings toward you. Body language signals happen on both a conscious and unconscious level.

We all subconsciously give away hints as to our true feelings, through our movements and gestures. Some important body gestures are as follows:

1. **Gesture:** Brisk, erect walk. **Meaning:** Confidence

2. **Gesture:** Standing with hands on hips. **Meaning:** Readiness, aggression

3. **Gesture:** Sitting with legs crossed, foot kicking slightly. **Meaning:** Boredom

4. **Gesture:** Sitting, legs apart. **Meaning:** Open, relaxed

5. **Gesture:** Arms crossed on chest. **Meaning:** Defensiveness

6. **Gesture:** Walking with hands in pockets, shoulders hunched **Meaning:** Dejection

7. **Gesture:** Hand to cheek. **Meaning:** Evaluation or thinking

8. **Gesture:** Touching, slightly rubbing nose. **Meaning:** Rejection, doubt or lying

9. **Gesture:** Rubbing the eye. **Meaning:** Doubt or disbelief

10. **Gesture:** Hands clasped behind back. **Meaning:** Anger, frustration, apprehension

11. **Gesture:** Locked Ankles. **Meaning:** Apprehension

12. **Gesture:** Head resting in hand, eyes downcast. **Meaning:** Boredom

13. **Gesture: Rubbing Hands. Meaning:** Anticipation

14. **Gesture:** Sitting with hands clasped behind head, legs crossed. **Meaning:** Confidence, superiority.

15. **Gesture:** Open palms. **Meaning:** Sincerity, openness, innocence

16. **Gesture:** Pinching bridge of nose, eyes closed. **Meaning:** Negative evaluation

17. **Gesture:** Tapping or drumming fingers. **Meaning:** Impatience

18. **Gesture:** Stapling fingers. **Meaning:** Authoritative

19. **Gesture:** Patting/fondling hair. **Meaning:** Lack of self confidence, insecurity

20. **Gesture:** Quickly tilted head. **Meaning:** Interest

21. **Gesture:** Stroking Chin. **Meaning:** Trying to make a decision

22. **Gesture:** Looking down, face turned away. **Meaning:** Disbelief

23. **Gesture:** Biting nails. **Meaning:** Insecurity, nervousness

24. **Gesture:** Pulling or tugging at ear. **Meaning:** Indecision

25. **Gesture:** Prolonged tilted head. **Meaning:** Boredom

## *Speech Improvement*

**<u>Pronunciation, Stress, Accent:</u>**

**(i) Clear Pronunciation:** the first important prerequisite of effective oral communication is that words should be pronounced clearly and correctly. Oral messages are often misunderstood because the speaker doesn't talk distinctly. Inability to use the jaws freely, to speak with a limber tongue and limber lips, and to speak slowly often makes for poor oral transmission. If a person tries to talk as fast as he thinks, his words will run to gather and get rammed into one another, so that when he intends asking 'what did you have?' He will succeed only in saying 'wajuhave?'

**(ii) Appropriate Word Choice:** Words have different meanings for different people. So it is important to be careful in the choice of words. The speaker, while speaking something, knows what he means, so he presumes that his listener also does so, which may be a wrong presumption. In oral communication it is more important to use the terms familiar to the listener rather than the terms that are familiar to the speaker.

**(iii) Natural Voice:** Some speakers deliberately cultivate an affected style under the impression that it would make them look more sophisticated. Nothing is farther from truth, and nothing impresses so much as the natural way of speech. One of the manuals for office employees in an American firm says, "The most effective

speech is that which is correct and at the same time natural and unaffected. Try to tone down an unusual accent and discard all affectations of speech. Try to cultivate a pleasing voice and speak clearly and distinctly."

## *Importance of Speech in Hotels:*

Good communication has many advantages for a business: strong communication:

- Motivates employees – helps them feel part of the business (see below).
- Easier to control and coordinate business activity – prevents different parts of the business going in opposite directions.
- Makes successful decision making easier for managers– decisions are based on more complete and accurate information.
- Better communication with customers will increase sales.
- Improve relationships with suppliers and possibly lead to more reliable delivery.

**Importance of speech in hospitality Industry**: The hospitality industry is a very fast-paced environment that deals with people on a daily basis. Hospitality staffs are not sitting behind a computer sending emails; they are interacting with customers every minute. Customers expect to receive exceptional service when staying at a hotel, visiting a restaurant, or flying on a plane. Without communication, this is not possible.

**Communication with Customers:**

The first critical part of communication in the hospitality industry is the communication with customers. The hospitality industry is also known as the service industry. In order to provide service to customers, there has to be communication. Customers have to communicate with service staff in order to make reservations for hotels, airlines, and restaurants. The service professionals in the hospitality industry need to be able to speak to customers and provide information.

For example, when checking into a hotel, if there is not clear communication with the customer, then the customer will not know where their room is located or how to get there. This needs to be communicated to them when they check in.

Also, if a customer has an issue, it is vital that the service staff communicate effectively in order to resolve the issue. For example, let's say that you are at a restaurant and your order is incorrect. The server needs to communicate to you that they are going to fix the situation and apologize for the error. If the server is not able to communicate properly in this situation, it could cause bigger issues.

**<u>Communication with Co-workers:</u>**

In addition to communicating with the customer, the staff and management need to be able to communicate with each other as well. In our example about the restaurant, the situation could have been a communication error that caused the wrong order to be served. It could have been avoided if proper communication was used between the server and the kitchen staff.

Also, managers will find that if proper communication is used between staff and management, they will have a better working atmosphere. If the information is not communicated to the staff, they may become frustrated with their jobs. For example, let's say that a restaurant keeps running out of items on the menu. If the servers are not told about these items, it can become frustrating for them when they are serving tables. This is why it is important for everyone to communicate in order to make it more efficient for both the staff and the customers.

***<u>There are two key elements of good communication across the board:</u>***

**<u>1. Training</u>**

The first tip is to make sure the staff is provided with proper training. For example, restaurants need to make sure the staff is trained on the menu so they can communicate with the customers about it. If a customer has a question about a menu item, the staff will not be able to explain it if they have not been trained properly. Hotels need to train their staff on the aspects of the hotel, including the location of rooms, restaurants, pools, and anything else they might need to explain to a customer.

**<u>2. Clear and Concise</u>**

In the hospitality industry, it is also important to keep communication clear and concise, whether dealing with the customers or the staff. If a restaurant server talks for twenty minutes about the specials, the chances are that the customer will be overwhelmed and forget what was said. If management holds long meetings with detailed information, the staff might not retain all of it. These situations are why it is important to keep communication clear and concise.

### **Common phonetic difficulties:**

Spelling words in English is challenging work. As a matter of fact, many native speakers of English have problems with spelling correctly. One of the main reasons for this is that many, many English words are NOT spelled as they are spoken. This difference between pronunciation and spelling causes a lot of confusion. The combination "ough" provides an excellent example:

- Tough - *pronounced - tuf (the 'u' sounding as in 'cup')*
- Through - *pronounced - throo*
- Dough - *pronounced - doe (long 'o')*
- Bought - *pronounced - bawt*

### **Most Important Rules for Avoiding Common Spelling Mistakes**

It's enough to make anyone crazy! Here are some of the most common problems when spelling words in English.

### *Three Syllables Pronounced as Two Syllables*

- Aspirin - *pronounced - asprin*
- Different - *pronounced - diffrent*
- Every - *pronounced - evry*

### *Four Syllables Pronounced as Three Syllables*

- Comfortable - *pronounced - comfrtable*
- Temperature - *pronounced - temprature*
- Vegetable - *pronounced - vegtable*

### *Words That Sound the Same (Homophones)*

- two, to, too - *pronounced - too*
- knew, new - *pronounced - niew*
- through, threw - *pronounced - throo*
- not, knot, naught - *pronounced - not*

### *Same Sounds - Different Spellings*
### 'Eh' as in 'Let'

- let

- bread
- said

**'Ai' as in 'I'**

- I
- sigh
- buy
- either

The following letters are silent when pronounced.

- **D** - sandwich, Wednesday
- **G** - sign, foreign
- **GH** - daughter, light, right
- **H** - why, honest, hour
- **K** - know, knight, knob
- **L** - should, walk, half
- **P** - cupboard, psychology
- **S** - island
- **T** - whistle, listen, fasten
- **U** - guess, guitar
- **W** - who, write, wrong

***Unusual Letter Combinations***

- **GH = 'F'**: cough, laugh, enough, rough
- **CH = 'K'**: chemistry, headache, Christmas, stomach
- **EA = 'EH'**: breakfast, head, bread, instead
- **EA = 'EI'**: steak, break
- **EA = 'EE'**: weak, streak
- **OU = 'UH'**: country, double, enough

## *Connective drills exercises:*

### Stressing individual words incorrectly:

If you usually speak with native English speakers, this will be the number one reason why they misunderstand you. It's very hard for native English speakers to 'translate' a word spoken as 'caLENdar' to the way they would pronounce it, 'CALendar'.

Non-native English speakers don't have as much of a problem with this, and will probably still understand what you're trying to say.

Quick fix: Listen carefully to the way people around you pronounce their words. If you hear a pronunciation that is different from yours, check the dictionary (even if it's a common word) to be sure that you're stressing it correctly. Some commonly mis-stressed words that we hear (with proper stress in capitals) include: PURchase, COLleague, phoTOGraphy and ecoNOMic.

**<u>Stressing the wrong words in a sentence:</u>**

Remember that you can completely change the meaning of a sentence by stressing different words in that sentence. For example, you could say this sentence in a number of different ways:

"I didn't say we should drive this way."

If you stress **I**, you emphasize that taking that route wasn't your idea. On the other hand, if you stress **drive**, you emphasize the mode of transport.

If you don't pay close attention to the words that you stress, you could end up sending a completely different message than the one you intended.

Quick fix:
Think about placing added emphasis on the word that is most important to your meaning. You can add emphasis by lengthening the word, saying it slightly louder and/or changing the pitch of your voice slightly.

**<u>Pronouncing certain consonant sounds incorrectly:</u>**

If people are misunderstanding you, it could very well be due to you confusing what is called 'voiced' and 'unvoiced' sounds. You might substitute 'p' for 'b' or 't' for 'd', for example. These sounds are so easily confused because their only difference is whether or not you use your voice to produce them. If you aren't careful, you could be making mistakes like saying 'tuck' for 'duck' or 'pay' for 'bay'.

Quick fix:
Pay attention to how you use your voice when you speak. You should be able to feel the vibration of your vocal cords when you make voiced sounds (b, d, g, v, z, r, l, m, n, ng, dge, zh, and voiced th). You can also try to make lists of pairs of words that use the sounds you find challenging and practice

repeating those. Record yourself so you can hear whether you're making any progress.

### Mixing up short and long vowel sounds:

Vowel sounds, like consonant sounds, can also be confused easily. The main problem with vowels happens when you mix up long and short vowel sounds. For example, the long 'ee' sound in 'seat' with the short 'i' sound in 'sit.' If you confuse these sounds, you end up saying completely different words. This can get confusing in conversation and forces people to draw much more from the context of your speech than the speech itself.

### Quick fix:

Make practice word lists like the ones you made for the consonant sounds and practice the sounds that are difficult for you.

### Forgetting to finish your words:

Do you have a tendency to let your word endings drop? We often hear people drop the 'ed' ending off of words in the past tense, for example. This is a dangerous mistake because not only is your pronunciation wrong, but it also sounds like you're making a grammatical mistake. People could judge you based on this type of error.

### Quick fix:

Do everything you can to articulate your word endings. One exercise that might help is to move the word ending onto the front of the following word. This will only work if the following word begins with a vowel sound. For example, try saying 'talk tuh lot' instead of 'talked a lot'.

## *Introduction to frequently used foreign sounds:*

- **Ad nauseam:** From Latin meaning to a sickening degree. "Tom talked ad nauseam about the time he scored the winning run."
- **Bon voyage:** From French meaning has a nice trip. "We all shouted 'bon voyage' as Rosa left for her vacation."
- **Bona fide:** From Latin meaning genuine. "Emma's teacher was a bona fide expert in European history."
- **Carte blanche:** From French meaning unlimited authority. "As the owner of the store, Mr. Williamson had carte blanche regarding what merchandise to sell."
- **Caveat emptor:** From the Latin meaning let the buyer beware. "I learned what caveat emptor meant the hard way when I bought a bike that never

seemed to work right."

- **En masse**: From French meaning in a large group. "The fans left the football stadium en masse once the score became 42 to 0."
- **Fait accompli**: From French meaning established fact. "Luis was disappointed, but his losing the election for class president was a fait accompli."
- **Faux pas**: From French meaning a social blunder. "Elizabeth realized too late that not attending Susan's party was a faux pas."
- **Ipso facto**: From Latin meaning by the fact itself. "A teacher, ipso facto, is in charge of his or her class."
- **Modus operandi**: From Latin meaning method of operating. "My modus operandi when studying is to set very specific goals."
- **Persona non grata**: From Latin meaning an unacceptable person. "Sally was a persona non grata in our club because she wouldn't follow the rules."
- **Prima donna**: From Latin meaning a temperamental and conceited person. "Laura wasn't popular with the other girls because they considered her to be a prima donna."
- **Pro bono**: From Latin meaning done or donated without charge. "The lawyer's pro bono work with the homeless gave him a sense of personal satisfaction."
- **Quid pro quo**: From Latin meaning something for something, usually an equal exchange. "Helping Ian with his math was quid pro quo for the time Ian helped me mow the lawn."
- **Status quo**: From Latin meaning the existing condition. "Because he didn't like change, Bert always tried to maintain the status quo."

## *Successfully Surviving the Kitchen*

You me get selected in any of your preferred department. You may not want to work in the Kitchen Department. However, being in any corner of the hotel and not being able to tactfully and bravely handle the Kitchen department will shorten your career in the hospitality industry. Hence the thing written below may help you like a life boat in the kitchen tornado.

Walking into a new kitchen for the first time can be an extremely scary thing. Each professional kitchen has its own culture and way of doing things. If you take one misguided step, you risk embarrassing yourself - not to mention possibly ending up in the dispensary with a chef-inflicted knife wound. To help you make a good first, and lasting impression, and to avoid costly doctor bills, here are the best and tested tips for surviving a professional kitchen.

### 1) Always Stay Calm.

This is much easier said than done. Professional kitchens are extremely high stress environments and it takes discipline and nerves of steel not to freak out. When someone the kitchen is nervous, it makes all the chefs nervous as well. We can smell your fear like a pack of wild dogs tracking an injured animal. Even if you're freaking out on the inside, you need to project a calm exterior; this will show that you have confidence in yourself and your abilities. Also, it's not your job to start screaming at one of your fellow cooks or the wait staff. (Let the Chef handle that one.)

### 2) Move Deliberately And With Efficiency.

This point cannot be over stressed. In a professional kitchen efficiency of movement is the key. A dead giveaway that you're a "Shoemaker" is when you start running around the kitchen like a damned chicken with its head cut off. Take a moment to collect your thoughts, gather your product for prep, and cut out any unnecessary movements. Here's a tip: anytime you have to pick something up or put it down, that's considered a step. Break your production into small steps to minimize movement and maximize speed and efficiency.

### 3) Always Ask For Clarification.

If you're not clear on a task that has been assigned to you, ASK! Sure, if you make a habit of this, it will probably annoy the chef off because it shows that you're not paying attention. However, the worst thing you can do is to be unsure about a task or technique and end up preparing the food wrong. Great kitchens are all about consistency. Trust me; you're much less likely to get smacked upside the head with a hot saute pan when asking for clarification than for damaging the chef's food.

### 4) Don't Pretend You Know More Than You Do.

Don't boast people about your knowledge or experience. If anything, you need to under promise and over deliver. Professional cooks and chefs are an extremely egotistical bunch; there's a lot of pompous talk about talent and knowledge. Learn to walk-the-walk before you talk-the-talk. Also, stop trying to impress people with French culinary terms. If they're applicable in the conversation, then use them. However, don't start throwing out some terminology to try and impress the chef. He'll be plenty impressed if you can learn the food and produce a consistent product.

### 5) Be Aware of Your Surroundings.

A kitchen is a crowded, hectic place. Let people know where you are at all times. Yell "corner" when walking around a corner. Say "Behind You" when walking behind someone. Say "Sharp" if you're walking by someone with a sharp knife and say "Hot" if you're walking around the kitchen with a hot pot. Not adhering to these rules is considered rude and dangerous, not to mention that it's a dead giveaway that you haven't spent much time in a professional kitchen. For a seasoned pro, these "call outs" are second nature. Chefs have been known to body check cooks into stoves when they try and walk behind them on the hotline without saying "Behind."

### 6) Do Your Homework.

Most restaurants have web pages complete with their menus. Read the menu and do research on any terms or dishes that you're not familiar with. Also, Google the restaurant name and the Executive Chef's name and read any article or web page to better understand what you're getting yourself into. This should be done before you even apply for the job. Make sure you're familiar with the restaurant, their food, and the chef's reputation before stepping foot into a new kitchen.

### 7) Shut Up.

When you first start in a new kitchen, try not to talk unless spoken to, or ask a direct question about the food or the current task at hand. Learn the cultural dynamics of the kitchen before you open your mouth and make a fool of yourself. The easiest way to alienate yourself on the first day of your new job is by being a "Chatty Cathy". If you want to gain the chef's favour, keep your mouth shut, work hard, and follow the tips in this article.

### 8) Be Clean and Organized.

Always keep your station clean and organized, and be sure to put everything in its proper place before moving onto another task. Keep all your product organized around your work station, and try to keep your jacket and apron as clean as possible. You can usually identify the pecking order of any kitchen by how dirty the aprons and jackets are. The dirtier the jacket, the lower down the totem pole they usually are.

### 9) Limit Your Vices.

This may seem like a strange tip if you've never worked in a professional kitchen. The fact of the matter is, people who work in restaurants tend to be a hard-partying bunch. If you've spent any time in the industry, chances are you've seen your fair share of extremely talented individuals self destruct because of problems with alcohol and drug abuse. You'd be surprised how much of an advantage you'd have over other people in the industry if you're not constantly showing up to work hung over or drained from other forms of degenerate partying.

### 10) Have A Purpose.

Working in a professional kitchen requires so much time, effort, and energy that you will not last if you don't have a purpose for being there. Maybe it's to study under a great chef, or to see how the restaurant is managed. Whatever it is, make sure the restaurant you work at is moving you towards your culinary goals. You do have a goal, don't you? You better, because if you don't, you're doomed to be a miserable failure.

# The Author

**Dr. Anshumali Pandey** is a renowned & reliable name in the field of Education, Hospitality, Tourism and Tribal Food. He is a Teacher and Chef by profession, and also an Author, a Business Auditor, and an avid culinary traveller to the Indian Sub continental hinterlands. Dr. Anshumali Pandey is a Hospitality Educator (PhD) who specialises in Higher Education, Office Administration, Pay roll, HR, Labour Laws, Audit, and Procurement & Tender Process. He is an Author with 79 Publications consisting of 61 Books and 3 short stories.

His contribution and research in the field of Tribal Food, Tribal Tourism, Forest Tourism and Village Tourism in the form of research papers have brought several laurels to him. In 2018 the Ministry of Tourism, Govt of Indian duly recognised all this and awarded him with a National Appreciation certificate and memento.

The books written by **Dr Anshumali Pandey** are essentially a banquet arising from an experience of over 26 years of Professional life and have boiled down to crisp and accurate writing on his favourite subjects. Hospitality Sector champion requires to be a specialist in many fields and Dr Pandey is one of them. His knowledge is evident from the spectrum of subjects which he has chosen for his books so far, which ranges from being a specialist chef, to Master of Human resources, to Education and to love for children, and topped with Spirituality. For more than two decades Dr

Pandey has lived with his family in Western India in general and the Tribal belt of the union territory of Dadra & Nagar Haveli in particular. Most of his time is consumed in helping and understanding the Tribal and rural population of the region and writing scholarly articles and books on his vast area of interest.

**Books written by the Author are –**

1. Theory of Indian Cookery
2. Beauty and Irony of Silvassa Tourism
3. A Short Indian Food Story
4. Be Your Own Guide to Indian Cuisine
5. Cookery Fundamentals
6. History of Indian Food (2 Editions Printed)
7. The Great Indian Story Book for Children
8. Personal Budget: Easy Work Book
9. Online Classes Log Book
10. Dictionary Making Work Book for School Children
11. The Lazy Bed
12. Hindu Dharm (हिन्दू_धर्म) (In Hindi Language)
13. Where is my coffee?
14. Your First Job is Never your Last (Volume 1)
15. You are Almost There (Quick Fix Resume and Interview Hacks)
16. Working for the Enemy? - A lesson in Career Management
17. Public Speaking for the Young
18. A Date With Coffee
19. How to be The Best Hotel Front Office Employee
20. Diploma in Food Production, The complete Syllabus
21. Diploma in F&B Service, The Complete Syllabus
22. Diploma in Front Office, The Complete Syllabus
23. The Time to Speak is Now
24. Munshi Premchand (Short Stories in English)
25. The Housekeeping Department, Text Book
26. Hitchhiker's Guide to Trekking in Uttarakhand
27. Uttarakhand, A divine Land for a Reason
28. Bachhon ke liye rochak kahaniyan (बच्चों के लिए रोचक कहानियां) (In Hindi Language)
29. Basic Communication Skills of English

30. The Basic Office Organisation Book for Start-ups
31. Hospitality HRM
32. Hospitality Marketing
33. Bakery Ingredients and Tools
34. Human Resource Management for Indian Professionals
35. The process of LAWFULLY operating a Hospitality business in India
36. Indian Classical Sweets: History, Tradition and Recipes
37. History of India's Himalayan Cuisine: Classical Cookery of Kashmir, Laddakh, Jammu, Himachal, Lahaul, Spiti, Garhwal, Kumaon.
38. Vindu: Andhra Cuisine (Part 1 of South Indian Trilogy)
39. Saappadu: Tamil Cuisine (Part 2 of South Indian Trilogy)
40. Sadya: Malayali Cuisine (Part 3 of South Indian Trilogy)
41. South Indian Cuisine - The Researcher's Guide Book
42. The Ramayana for Children and other short stories from Indian Mythology
43. Legends of the Tribal Shiva
44. Third Generation Children's Story Book
45. It's Elementary: The Top Nine Adventures from the memoirs of Dr John H Watson
46. UNITY IN DIVERSITY, The foundation of Indian Tourism
47. The Thar Express: Culinary History of Rajasthan and Gujarat
48. Basics of Computerized Accounting
49. Impact (Impact of Globalization on Indian Social Life)
50. Vishnu – The Lord of Amazing Incarnations
51. Being a Mahatma in the Freedom Struggle
52. The Culinary Journey of Purvanchal: Lucknow to Patna
53. Culinary History of the Gangetic Plains
54. Indian Culinary Secrets
55. The Story of Jain and Parsi Food
56. The Great Indian Pilgrimage Tourism
57. Introduction to Tourism Studies – Text Book
58. Bread and Rolls
59. Diploma in Digital Marketing the Complete Syllabus
60. The Theory of Sweetened Bakery Foods
61. Campus Placement Guide for Management Trainee in Leading Hotels

Connect with me: anshumali.pandey@gmail.com
https://notionpress.com/author/337004

*Please scan this QR code on your phone to know more about the latest and complete works of Dr Anshumali Pandey*